Rollercoaster

Path to Islam

Na'ilah Cruz

Copyright Information & ISBN
979-8-9853028-0-6

Dedication

In loving memory of my Mom, a born survivor and true warrior who spent most of her life battling demons. Nosotras te honramos, Mama!

roll er coast er roll ər ˈkōstər

Noun
An amusement park attraction that consists of a light
railroad track with many tight turns and steep slopes,
on which people ride in small fast cars.

Verb
Move, change, or occur in the dramatically
changeable manner of a roller coaster.
An experience in which circumstances change rapidly
and in a volatile manner from one extreme to another.

Contents

Introduction vii

Chapter One - Earliest Memories of Mom and Dad 1

Chapter Two - Social Events and Restrictions........................11

Chapter Three - My First Love 17

Chapter Four - Mom's Abdominal Pain..................................26

Chapter Five - Funeral 32

Chapter Six - Blood and Water 38

Chapter Seven - Transitions..44

Chapter Eight - Job Corps 56

Chapter Nine - Southern Vermont College............................72

Chapter Ten - The Call 84

Chapter Eleven - The Path to Islam 94

Chapter Twelve - Journey to Hajj 105

Introduction

As a child I remember how whenever my dad returned from his job as a longshoreman, he would take us to Coney Island.

My dad's unspoken rule was to eat first, then explore the rides on the island.

Straight out of the subway, we headed to the nearest outdoor oyster bar, where my dad would loudly slurp down a few oysters. My oldest brother and I had one objective only: to explore the arcades and get on as many rides as possible.

The rollercoaster was the first ride I experienced,

Prior to being seated into the ride, I felt a combination of heart-thumping fear and a rush of excitement at the same time. As the cart began with a slow incline toward the top, butterflies of fear churned inside my stomach, followed by a sudden speedy plunge downward, meeting many quick tight turns, loops and steep slopes at a speed of 95 MPH, which produced a euphoric sense of freedom within me, replacing the fear and butterflies with exhilaration.

When the ride was over, my brother and I met my dad outside. I ran towards him, unable to contain my extreme excitement and elation over what I'd just experienced. I asked him if I could go on the ride again, and my dad's face lit up as he laughed at my eagerness to repeat the ride. Then he looked at my brother, whose face showed the complete opposite reaction to his experience. My dad asked my brother to go back on the ride with me, as my brother pleaded to my dad that he didn't want to go back on the rollercoaster.

Now, my dad is a strong Latin man and wasn't happy that his young daughter displayed more courage and bravery than his oldest son. He chided him about it.

Nonetheless, the rollercoaster became my all-time, go-to ride at any amusement park I attended.

Unbeknownst to me in my childhood, the rollercoaster rides I thoroughly enjoyed would become the metaphor of my entire life. Several turning points in my life have catapulted me into the seat of many a rollercoaster ride, a few of which involved insurmountable challenges, extreme danger, risk, and devasting loss.

By the end of this book, you will come to know in detail about these turning points and how each one ultimately gave me experiences that have shaped the intangible of who I am.

Chapter One

Earliest Memories of Mom and Dad

My dad froze when he first laid eyes on my mom as she and her friends were leaving the movie theatre. He raced up to her intending to introduce himself and possibly ask her on a date. Instead he looked into her eyes, then kissed her. Mom and her friends stood there in shock for a few seconds, trying to process whether they should open up a can of whoop-ass on him or compassionately escort him to Bellevue Psychiatric Hospital.

After Mom collected her thoughts, she pushed him away. Then she and her girlfriends started cursing him. His friends came to his rescue, and they ran into the theatre. The unmitigated gall and balls of my dad.

They ended up running into each other again a few weeks later at a bodega in the neighborhood where my mom lived. She was about to enter the bodega while Dad was coming out, his bicycle on the ground in front of the store. Dad couldn't contain his delight and stroke of good fortune to have a second opportunity to properly meet and speak with Mom.

She scowled at him defiantly and couldn't believe he was standing before her again. An eerie feeling came over her and she could feel her heart beating faster at the thought of him living in her neighborhood, too. She quickly walked past him to enter the store. "Excuse me, I would like to apologize for my behavior from a few weeks ago."

Mom looked at him, rolled her eyes, and went into the store. A few minutes later, as she left the store, there was my dad on his bike waiting for her. Three sons and one daughter later were the obvious conclusion when Mauricio Santos Cruz met Yvonne Elna Bennett.

My brother Phil is Mom and Dad's second son, born five years before me. He's 6'1, light-complexioned, and has a lean body. Phil played ice hockey in high school and other sports most of his life.

I would say, Phil has the most traits of my mom of any of my other siblings, including myself. He's gregarious like my mom and has a deep concern and loyalty to his family and close friends. He's also hysterically funny and is the life of the party anywhere he goes. He always dressed well and had the latest fashion in clothes and shoes. I would sneak into his bedroom and steal his shirts to wear.

When we were kids, I'm sure I annoyed him to no end. I was a little envious at the fact that he was a guy and could do and go anywhere he wanted. The gender standards were the same in our house as far as domestic activities: for example, cooking, cleaning and washing dishes. Mom was an equal opportunity enforcer in this area. However, when it came to curfew, allowances and social activities, there was a distinct difference between Phil and me.

He started working as a young teenager, and I believe his first job was at our neighborhood pharmacy as a cashier. I would get money if I needed it or most times, he would just give it to me. He was instrumental in getting us through a difficult time in our lives.

Although my brother Marlon was Mom and Dad's second oldest son, he died at six months. My mom's first-born son, my brother Randolph, wasn't raised with us. In fact, I met him for the first time when I was seven or eight years old. He came to visit us for a few days when we lived in Boston. I never saw him again after that day.

Kevin is Mom and Dad's third son, born exactly 18 months after me. Kev and I are similar in characteristics. He moved around independently like me. Kev is about 5'9, average weight, and I believe he and I had more traits of my dad than Mom. Kev is the fashion stylist of the family with a taste for caviar. He wears his clothes extremely well and always seems to have a pulse on what's new and or trending. He's extremely generous and thoughtful. He and I used to battle a lot. It probably had to do with the closeness in age.

Stephanie is mom's sixth and last-born child. Her dad was Leon. She is my younger sister and one of the few women I call my friend. She was a momma's girl. I remember Mom saying that everything she envisioned me to be as a daughter, she ended up getting when she gave birth to Steph. Steph was everything the opposite of me. She played with her dolls, wore cute, pink, frilly dresses and shoes, and stuck close to Mom. She didn't want to get messy, dirty, or play rough. Now might be a different story. She resembles Mom the most. She has Mom's caramel complexion and facial features, stands at about 5'5, and is shapely like Mom.

Ironically, she and I have a birthmark in the exact same place on our bodies. I would say she has her dad's cool, reserved demeanor.

I don't have clear memories of Mom and Dad doing things with us together as a family. We did specific things with Mom and whenever my dad was home, we ate dinner together as a family and went to the beach for picnics. Other times, Dad would take me and my brothers to Coney Island without Mom.

My mom was an enigma to me. I knew her, but I really didn't know her. She stood at about 5'5, with a beautiful caramel-brown complexion, and was nicely shaped. At times, she was a strong disciplinarian and at other times, she was the most compassionate, indulgent mother. What I did know about Mom was that in addition to her working two jobs, she always had a side hustle going on. During the week, she worked at a hospital or a nursing home. I watched her put on her nursing uniform and thought how pretty she looked, dressed in white with the nursing cap on her head to complete the look.

One of my first memories of seeing how much and how hard Mom worked was during a weeknight. My brothers and I were outside, playing in front of the house. It was 6 PM. I know this because the streetlamps would light up the block every night at this time.

I went inside the house to get a drink of water and saw Mom putting on her nurse uniform, which was odd to me because she usually wouldn't leave for work until 11 PM. As I walked into the kitchen, she looked at me with a stern expression, then asked, "Why are you kids still outside at almost 11 at night?"

"Mom, it's only 6," I said, puzzled and confused. I noted the bewildered look on her face, then she went into the dining room area to check the clock above the table. I watched her gaze at the clock for a few seconds, then she turned to me and laughed.

"I'm sorry, honey. When I woke up and saw it was dark, I thought I had overslept and would be running late for work." She kissed me and told me to remind my brothers to come inside by 9. I said, "Okay Mommy," as I left the kitchen and walked towards the front door. I stopped for a second and could see Mom in her room taking off her uniform and laying down on the bed. I don't think Mom realized at the time how working so hard was taking a toll.

On the weekends, Mom was a nanny to a white, wealthy couple that lived around the Central Park area in Manhattan. We lived in Brooklyn at the time, and she took two trains to get to her weekend job. I only remember meeting one of the children, a girl about the same age as me. Her name was Christine. One weekend, Mom took me to work with her and as we walked into the house, Christine met us at the door. She hugged Mom, and Mom said, "Christine, this is my daughter Misha."

"Do you want to see my room?" Christine smiled.

She escorted me to her room. When we got to the entrance, I gasped and stopped dead in my tracks. My eyes filled with joy and delight as I gazed at the gigantic spiraling slide in the center of her bedroom!

Christine ran to the back of the gigantic slide, climbed up the steps and when she got to the top, she sat down, raised her arms up, and shouted, "WHEEEEEEEE!" as she began sliding and spiraling down. When she finally got to the bottom of the slide, we simultaneously screamed with excitement and laughter. What else would two seven-year-old girls do?

It seemed we spent the entire night on that gigantic spiraling slide, taking turns going up and down repeatedly, with only the sound of pure joy, excitement, and laughter coming from the room. It was an unforgettable weekend.

***

I almost died as a toddler.

I got an infection after being given a vaccine that spiked my temperature to 105 for several days. Mom said the pediatrician tried everything to bring my temperature down, but nothing he did would break the high fever. Finally, he told Mom that I would not survive much longer with a dangerously high fever and that she should prepare herself. Mom understood what that meant. She left the hospital and went straight to her Catholic church nearby.

She told me she spent a few hours there, crying, lighting candles and kneeling at the altar, asking God to not take me away from her. Mom said she arrived back at the hospital after midnight. I was sleeping, and she placed her hand on my chest to make sure I was still breathing. The nurse said my temperature was the same. She sat on the recliner near my bed and fell asleep.

She woke up to see several nurses and the pediatrician hovering over me. Mom's heart thumped. She stood up and held her breath as she looked at me, then at the pediatrician. He turned towards Mom with a solemn expression, gently smiled, and said, "Her temperature is 99.8." Mom couldn't control the tears and she hugged the pediatrician and the nurses.

When they left the room, she picked me up and placed me on her lap as she sat down on the recliner. She thanked God for answering her prayers, then she said she rocked me in her arms for a few minutes. I opened my eyes and smiled at her. She kissed and squeezed me tightly, looked at me, and said, "God must have some specific purpose for you."

Mom told me this story when I was nine-years-old. This wouldn't be the only time in my life that I had a near death experience.

It was common during the summer for us to frequent our neighborhood recreation center and swim in the pool. One day, Mom accompanied me and my brother Phil to the pool. I was 10 or 11-years-old and didn't know how to swim, and so I would always go to the shallow end of the pool. We had never been to this particular pool, and I walked to the area which I thought was the shallow end, and jumped in.

I learned quickly that I was in the deep end and sunk to the bottom. I screamed, "I'm drowning! Help! Help!" as my arms flapped. I felt the weight of my body pulling downward and had gulped a lot of water. I heard someone yell, "Save her, she's too fat!" In that moment, a flash of me drowning came over me and my entire body sank towards the bottom of the pool.

The only thing I remember after that was opening my eyes and someone leaning over me to perform CPR. My mom was next to me and so were a bunch of other people. That experience prompted me to take swimming lessons to ensure that I would be able to swim in any body of water thereafter. Today, I'm a pretty good swimmer.

I was an overweight kid, got teased a lot, and was made fun of. Some kids in school used to call me "chugamug." I didn't know what a chugamug was, but it sounded and gave me a visual of a hideous, obese entity.

I started writing in my diary during this time. I was 12. My diary became my closest friend, companion, and an outlet to express my every thought, emotion, and secrets. I wrote in my diary all the time and I enjoyed spending time writing about everything. It also provided a way for me to be independent of needing to have friends and to be okay with my own company. My early writing helped me in ways I'm only understanding now as an adult; it promoted my personal growth and development.

I was an extreme tomboy and wanted to do everything my brother Phil did and go everywhere he went. Instead of having tea parties with my dolls that stayed in pristine condition on my bed, I was out learning how to ride a bike, make slingshots out of wire hangers, and play the Skully board game, a board drawn on a flat surface, a pavement or playground, where we sent bottle caps gliding into a box. These were some of the activities that boys did, and it was more fun to me than anything girls liked doing.

My brother Phil got a job at the local skating arena, and I became obsessed with all things that had to do with skating. At first, it wasn't a pretty sight. I fell in the worst possible ways one can fall while learning how to rollerskate, but I kept at it. We would go to the rink at least two or three times a week and on weekends, too.

Phil looked like a professional skater. He skated really fast, skated backwards, and did a variety of tricks. I was determined to be just as good as my brother. Mom bought me skates, and I decorated them with big colorful pom-pom's. It wasn't long before I started doing tricks, skating fast and backwards too.

The Utica skating arena in Brooklyn had a social vibe and

energy that you felt as soon as you entered. The music was loud and kept you constantly on the floor moving, shaking, and perfecting your skating skills.

Skating was the activity that caused me to drop all the excess weight from my body. Suddenly, my clothes started falling off me and Mom had to take me shopping for new clothes. Besides the weight loss, I noticed boys started talking to me more and asking me if I wanted to play Skully or ride our bikes to the park. Some of the older guys on our block would call me by my name and say hello. Some would say, "Girl, you gonna break some hearts when you get older!" I had no idea what they meant at the time. All I knew was that it seemed everyone wanted to either talk to me or be my friend, especially boys, after my weight loss.

My dad was away from home for most of my life. He wasn't a tall man, but he had a quiet, cool demeanor about him. He wore a fedora on his head, Ray-Ban sunglasses, and sometimes I'd see him with a cigarette in his hand and at other times a cigar. I was told by a relative that Dad was a phenomenal dancer and would command much attention at any social events he attended.

He was always neat in his appearance. Well-organized and well-mannered in public was a standard for himself and his children. Mom and Dad often received compliments on how well-behaved and mannered we were.

Dad also was a drinker and would go through bouts of binge drinking that would cause him to miss weeks of work at a time. He remained in his job until his retirement despite these episodes.

When I got older and understood what binge drinking was, I wondered what caused my dad to drink in that way. What was he trying to escape from by drinking himself to death? Dad was a longshoreman and worked at the docks and commercial ports in Brooklyn and Manhattan. He loaded and unloaded cargo onto ships; he also operated machinery. At the time, I was under the impression that his job caused him to be at sea for long periods of time, which would have explained his not being home much.

The truth of the matter was my dad had another family.

I didn't learn about his son and two daughters, all older than myself and my three brothers, until I was fifteen years old. I only met his son briefly, also named Mauricio. I was never told about these older siblings by Mom, Dad, or any of our relatives. The details about my dad's other family remain a mystery, which made him an enigma to me too.

Chapter Two

Social Events and Restrictions

My parents were very social people, especially Mom. The house she purchased on 287 East 93RD Street in Brooklyn was where I had the fondest memories. The weekends that Mom didn't work her second job, she hosted domino and card games in our basement that held 25 or more people. She would set up the basement with rows of chairs and tables, and a bar.

Mom cooked a lot of different foods to serve and sell. Her ethnic food specialty was Tamales, a typical Spanish dish made with a corn-based dough mixture that could be filled with meat and vegetables, wrapped inside foil and steamed until fully cooked. Delish! They always sold out, and some people would pre-order for the following week. Hosting the games and selling food was one of Mom's side hustles, in addition to betting on horses and playing numbers. She also hosted and sold Tupperware a few days during the week before going to work at night.

I remember how lively our house used to be with the different social events. We heard music playing and the loud voices coming from downstairs. I don't know how I was able to fall asleep. The domino games lasted the entire weekend, with some people playing from Saturday until Sunday morning and others not leaving our basement until Monday at 6 AM.

Our individual birthday parties were spectacular and brought the most people to our home, including children and adults. The guests were a mixture of family, friends, co-workers, and those who lived in our neighborhood. Mom invited anyone to come and partake in our festivities; she was a natural at preparing, hosting, and managing an event or party. She decorated the entire house to mark the event, too. She had our birthday cakes custommade from an upscale bakery, and the cakes were stunning. One year she had a merry-go-round cake made for me or Steph, I can't remember, but I do recall that the cake was massive, and they operated it to move like a real merry-go-round. It mesmerized the children in attendance, including us. Other cakes included one designed to look like a train with moving tracks and another that was a tower made of M&Ms.

In the evening, the child's birthday party transitioned to a party for the adults. All the children would either play in front of the house, or remain on the first floor. The basement was reserved for the adults.

I remember going into my mom's bedroom and seeing a massive amount of birthday presents covering her bed. It was a kid's delight to see, and we all received really nice, expensive gifts. We just didn't always know who they were from.

Once, I came home from school and the living room door was closed. I was about to open it when Mom said to me, "Wait, I want to take you somewhere, but you'll need to change your school clothes."

"Where are we going?" I asked as I walked away from the living room door.

Her face lit up. "It's a surprise. I put a light blue dress on your bed, put that on."

I went to my room and changed into a light blue dress, then went to the kitchen. Mom looked at me and said, "You look beautiful!"

"I love the color of the dress," I smiled.

She looked proudly at me and said, "You have the most beautiful smile, Meesh." I hugged her, then she took me into the bathroom to comb my hair.

On the way out the door, she grabbed her handbag, then just as we were about to exit through the kitchen she said, "Oh, I left my wallet in the living room on the coffee table. Go get it for me, please."

"Okay, Mom."

I walked back to the living room door, opened it, and heard a loud, "Surprise!" I saw about eight or ten of my friends from school and the neighborhood dressed nicely with party hats on. I greeted everyone and asked them why they were there. Before they could answer, I looked over at the table and it was decorated with party streamers, place mats, and a porcelain teapot at the center of the table, with individual teacups and saucers on each placemat. There were mini Bundt cakes lined up neatly near the teapot, along with an assortment of teas. I saw small, triangle turkey-and-cheese sandwiches, chips, and a variety of fruit. I was pleasantly surprised and overjoyed.

At that moment, Mom came into the living room. Grinning, I rushed over to her and gave her the biggest squeeze. She explained that one weekend she had worked at the wealthy couple's home in Central Park where she helped prepare a tea party the couple planned for their daughter Christine. So Mom decided she would do the same for me.

It was so grand. The rest of that day could not have been more perfect and complete. My friends and I laughed, ate, and pretended to be cultured, snobby socialites as we picked up our teacups, sticking out our pinky fingers as we drank.

Mom's ideas about rearing children were strict and involved some religious restrictions. My mother truly believed in cultivating children with good manners and behavior. We were reared to say, "Please" and "Thank you" to people, and if an adult addressed you regarding any subject, the response from us was always to include "Ma'am" and "Sir." We weren't allowed to be in the company of adults while they were talking. We automatically left the area if Mom received a phone call or if another adult was present. After saying hello, we understood that it was time to leave. We implemented this unspoken rule without hesitation. We had to be on our very best behavior in public and while visiting people.

We were also not allowed to question a decision. Don't you dare roll your eyes, suck your teeth, or have a tantrum. That was considered blatant disrespect and would not be tolerated. The consequence brought punishment by whatever was within Mom's reach: a shoe flung in your direction, or a few taps with a wooden spoon, a leather belt, and on a rare occasion, depending on the severity of the offense, a lash from an extension cord.

If we were getting out of sorts, Mom gave us a look, and we instantly adjusted ourselves. She was not in the least afraid or hesitant to discipline us if she had to. She told us that if we did something that warranted her to discipline us she would do so even if it were in front of the police station or a judge. She meant every word and would act swiftly to prove it.

Mom would not allow us to sleep over at other people's homes. She was adamant on this issue. She welcomed our friends to come and stay over at our house, but we could not stay overnight at theirs.

Sitting on the steps in front of the house or building, even playing near the fire hydrant during the summer, was also taboo. We used to take the lid off the hydrant so that when the water gushed out, it pushed us along the street. Mom considered these actions to be low and what street people did. In her mind, she was rearing us, not dragging us through the streets. I wasn't allowed to wear spaghetti-strapped shirts or shorts above my knees. Mom always kept us close to her. She had a watchful eye whether she was around or not and always seemed to know what was happening with us. I always felt like she kept an extra watchful eye on me, as if she wanted to keep me safe and out of harm's way. I am grateful for my mom's protectiveness and some of the strict rules enforced because I honestly believe it saved us from encounters with unsuspecting predators.

Our family was Catholic, and Mom tried to instill those religious values in us through practical application. There was a specific night dedicated to Bible reading and study. We sat at the table and each of us took turns reading a passage. Then Mom asked us questions about what we read to check our understanding, and we closed each session with a prayer.

She made a point to teach and help us know about God. We went to church on Sundays and, if she couldn't attend, she made sure Phil and I went. Occasionally, we would go and sit through the entire sermon just to be able to tell Mom the topic for that week and, of course, to receive the wafer and wine. Other times, Phil and I would skip church completely and hang out for an hour. We never got caught, which increased our heedless ways.

I've always believed in God, but clearly had doubts about some aspects of the Catholic faith. I wanted to know why I had to confess to the priest about my sins or mistakes so that he could act as an intermediary between me and God. Why couldn't I just speak to God directly about what I did and ask for forgiveness for myself? The concept of the trinity still confuses me to this day. However, Mom was good about answering any questions I had on the subject.

Chapter Three

My First Love

"When I first fell in love, I didn't know what hit me! Bang! Smash! Crash!"

The first time I heard this lyric in Janet Jackson's song, *Control*, I laughed because it described exactly what I experienced when I first saw Will.

We lived at 596 Maple St in the Crown Heights section in Brooklyn. I was walking out of my house when I looked up and suddenly stopped breathing. In slow motion, I watched these two guys walk past my house.

One was tall, about 6'3, dark-skinned, athletically built, wore a three-quarter tan colored leather jacket, a brown mock neck shirt and jeans. I could not move or take my eyes off him. They went inside my neighbor's house a few feet away.

Who and what was that? I wondered. I'd never had that kind of reaction to seeing a guy. I carried on with my day and didn't think much of it afterwards.

A week later, I was visiting some neighbors, Gloria and Heather, who lived a few houses down. They invited me to play cards with them and a few other friends. I got to their house, greeted everyone, and we started to play the card game. About half an hour later, the doorbell rang. Their mom asked me to answer the door, so I got up from the couch and went into the hallway. I saw the silhouette of two guys and when I got closer to the door, I recognized them as the same two guys who had walked past my house. I panicked and wanted to run back inside, but it was too late. I opened the door and greeted them.

"Hi," they both smiled. "Are Gloria and Heather here?" Will asked.

"Yes, they're inside."

They followed me inside, and the butterflies fluttered.

Once we all got settled, we continued playing cards, and everyone was talking and joking around during the game. Will and his friend talked the most with Gloria, Heather, and even their brother, Steve. I was quiet most of the time, avoiding eye contact with Will. After an hour, Will and his friend got up and left. I felt relieved and disappointed that I didn't say anything to him, nor did he directly say anything to me. As I gathered my things to leave, Heather said to me, "Will asked Steve questions about you."

"Asking questions about me? What kind of questions did he ask?" I sat on the sofa in anticipation.

"He asked what your name was and where you live and if he could have your number."

I stopped breathing again. Was this a joke? Did he really ask her brother those questions about me? He didn't appear to have any interest in me at all when they were there.

"Do you want to give your number? Heather asked. "He's going to call my brother tomorrow to find out."

I was quiet for a few minutes. I wanted him to have my number, but I also felt nervous about speaking with him.

Finally, I looked at Heather and said, "Yes."

She laughed, then gave her brother my number.

The next day at 4 PM, my house phone rang. The butterflies returned, and I just stared as the phone rang a third time. Finally I grabbed it, placed the receiver to my ear and said, "Hello."

"Hi, is Misha home?" It was him.

My heart started beating, and all I heard for a split second was, "Bang! Smash! Crash!"

"Yes, this is Misha."

"Thank you for letting me speak with you," he said. "When I saw you walk towards the door to let us inside, my heart stopped beating! You're a very pretty girl. I wanted to speak with you yesterday, but I was nervous. I thought if I got close enough to you, then I would be able to start a conversation, but as I sat near you, I suddenly felt butterflies churning in my stomach."

I was dumbfounded and could not believe what I was hearing.

"Are you okay?"

I was silent for most of the conversation.

"I'm okay."

"Would you like to go to a movie over the weekend?"

I agreed. He asked for my address and told me the time he would pick me up. I was floating on air for the rest of the day.

On the day of our date, I asked him to pick me up at my neighbor's house, because my mom would have killed me if he rang our doorbell. I was under 17 years old when I met him, and I was not allowed to date or even have boys call my house. He agreed but asked me the reason why he couldn't pick me up from my house. I told him I would explain later.

He arrived at my neighbor's on time. I heard the doorbell ring and the butterflies in my stomach fluttered furiously.

When I went to the door, there he stood, tall and very handsome with roses in his hand. I welcomed him, smiling, and he handed me the roses. "I hope you like roses."

"They're beautiful, thank you."

He was the perfect gentleman during the entire date. He opened the car door for me, walked closely, but didn't touch me. I started to feel calm and relaxed in his presence. The butterflies subsided. I felt comfortable.

After the movie, we went to a restaurant and had lunch. He asked me why he had to pick me up at the neighbors. I explained that my mom was Catholic and had strict rules and I wasn't allowed to have a boyfriend, date or even have a boy call my house. He looked puzzled.

"I understand and respect your mom's religious beliefs, but I don't understand why a 17- or 18-year-old couldn't at least talk to boys over the phone."

I was silent and looked away from him. He became silent too, like he was reading the reason for my silence.

"How old are you?"

I felt a knot of tension in the pit of my stomach and thought carefully before responding. Should I lie and say I'm 19 or tell him the truth? I believed telling him the truth would run him out of the restaurant. I made my decision, took a breath, and said, "I'm under 17."

"You're under 17?" He sat back in his seat, staring at me.

He was 19 years old and even though only a few years

separated us, I was under 17 and that was the major difference. He leaned forward in his seat, smiled and said, "The way you carry yourself, your maturity, made me think you were closer to my age. Now I understand why your mom put restrictions on you dating. She's trying to protect her underaged daughter."

My heart sank, and the knots in my stomach increased. I just knew that this would be the last date and the last time I would see him.

I looked down into my plate as he spoke. He moved his chair beside me, turned and pulled my chair close to face him. He looked into my eyes. "I want to protect and keep you safe too, Misha, and so we're going to take this real slow." He kissed me on my forehead. Pure calm came over my whole body, and in that instant, I felt safe.

He took me back home and told me he would call me tomorrow. I walked into my house, went to my room, and pulled out my diary. I think I spent the entire night writing every detail of my date with Will.

We continued to spend a lot of time together, and after six months of dating, Will asked me to go with him to Downstate Medical hospital in Brooklyn so that we could get information about the various birth control methods. I felt nervous and excited at the same time because my feelings continued to grow for him and I wanted to have my first sexual experience with him. He told me while we waited for the nurse to present the contraception options that he didn't want us to make a mistake and have a baby before I finished H.S or marriage, and so he thought to do the responsible thing by getting us to use birth control. After watching the videos and looking over some of the literature, I decided on using the pills. They were convenient and the least invasive. A week later, we were intimate. Will talked me through the entire act from beginning to end slowly and he was so delicate and mindful of every step, making sure that I was comfortable and feeling good. I literally felt made love to, the experience was euphoric, and I fell even deeper in love with him. During this time, I also met all his family and he met my siblings. They all liked him; Mom was the only one that didn't know he existed.

One day he picked me up and took me over to his brother's house for lunch, where he announced that he had enlisted in the U.S Air Force and would be leaving for basic training in two months.

His family congratulated him, especially his brother, who had served a four-year term in the Army, and they also had another brother who served in the Marines. I was happy and sad at the same time, but told him I was proud of him. We stayed at his brother's house for a few hours, playing cards, talking and having a good time, until he took me back home.

"You are in big trouble!" Phil said to me as he entered my bedroom. Mom found your diary and read everything you wrote about Will." I went pale.

"Oh my God! She's going to kill me."

Before he or I could say another word, my mom walked into my room with my diary in her hand. Phil hurriedly left. What a punk, I thought, not staying there to support me. I froze, waiting for the moment she would take my head off. I didn't see rage or even anger on her face. Instead, she handed me my diary and told me I was grounded and could not leave the house except to go to school and back for a week. She turned around and walked out of my room.

I was pleasantly shocked and confused. This was not a typical response of my mom when a rule was violated, especially when the rule was of this magnitude. I was curious about her response and grateful I still had my head and life intact, but still curious.

I spoke with my boyfriend the next day and told him what had happened. He told me everything would be okay and not to worry. We didn't see each other for the week I was grounded.

Mom worked nights, and she usually returned home around 7 AM. This particular morning when she came home, my siblings and I were getting ready for school. Mom quickly made breakfast, and we all sat at the table to eat.

"Something happened last night when I was waiting for the bus on my way to work," Mom said. "I was at the bus stop when this tall, handsome, well-dressed, and well-mannered young man approached me and asked if I was Ms. Bennett. I smiled at the young man and said 'Yes.' I asked him if I knew him or his parents but he said no. Then he introduced himself and told me that he was in love with you." Mum looked directly at me. "He said he wants to marry you after you finish high school."

My brother Phil kicked me under the table, and once again, I froze. My boyfriend is going to get me killed, I thought. Why did he do this? And why didn't he ask or tell me he would do this?

Mom looked over at me from across the table. "I've invited him for dinner to get to know him better."

I thought, What? She invited my boyfriend that I'm not supposed to have for dinner to get to know him better!

I couldn't have been more relieved that my boyfriend was no longer a secret, and more importantly, my mom was warming up and even accepting him as such. He came for dinner a week later and everything went smoothly. Mom talked with him about his family and his future plans. He told her he was going into the military in a few weeks and would have a better sense of which profession to choose once he established himself there.

Mom seemed pleased with everything he said. She served us dessert, and we all moved into the living room to watch TV. He asked Mom if he could sit next to me on the couch, and Mom smiled and gave a nod. I knew right then that she not only liked him, but she trusted him with me. It was a great evening and for the first time ever, I saw my mom let herself be open to change.

The day had come. My boyfriend was leaving for bootcamp in less than 12 hours. He came to my house earlier in the day to take me with him while he ran his errands. We spent every minute of the time he had left together. After running around, we went to visit all of his siblings. He had five brothers, one sister, and a bunch of nephews and nieces. We saw aunts, uncles and his grandfather. Everyone was so happy and proud of him; the love showed in each one of them.

It was midnight when he pulled up in front of my house. His flight was scheduled to leave at 4 AM. He came inside my house and we sat on the couch in the living room. Mom was at work and my siblings were asleep. We talked about our future and reminisced for an hour, then he said, "It's time, baby."

He stood up. My heartbeat quickly as I rose from the couch. He lightly grabbed the front of my blouse and pulled me close to him, then wrapped his arms around the middle of my back and squeezed me tightly. Strong emotions filled my heart, and tears poured down my cheeks. I think he felt what I was feeling too and continued squeezing me closer and tighter against his body like a protective shield.

He loosened his grip and pulled me back gently to look at my face. "I love you, Misha. I'll be back in a few weeks. Wait for me."

"I love you too. Of course, I'll wait for you," I replied. Then he squeezed me one more time and kissed me. As he walked out the door he said, "See you soon, baby."

"See you soon." I literally felt my heart break and couldn't control the tears. I went over to the window and watched him get into his car. He didn't leave right away. He just sat in the car for about ten minutes, then drove off.

Chapter Four

Mom's Abdominal Pain

Mom complained of abdominal pain for a few weeks.

I don't remember much about what happened in the weeks prior to those complaints. What I do remember was that at the end of May, a week before she contacted her doctor, she appeared to be losing weight. It wasn't unusual because Mom's weight often fluctuated. She was always trying different diets and at home, she exercised with Jack Lalanne in the morning a few times a week and so I had attributed her weight loss to that.

Will returned from boot camp at the end of May as well.

It was the first time seeing him again since he left in early March. He was to be home for two weeks before returning. His aunt Alice went to pick him up from JFK airport. His cousins and an old girlfriend/friend of the family and I waited at his aunt's house. We decorated the living room with colorful streamers and had a variety of food and drinks, buffet-style, in the kitchen.

I was feeling the butterflies in my stomach as if it was the first time meeting him. In some ways, it was like the first time meeting him because I expected that he must have changed somewhat after experiencing boot camp and military life. The anticipation was exhausting, yet exciting.

We heard the key in the door and scrambled to turn off the lights. We heard him and Aunt Alice talking, then as they walked into the living room, the lights came on and we shouted, "Surprise!" He started laughing and everyone ran over to greet and hug him. I stayed distant, observing how handsome he looked in his blue uniform. I instantly became calm upon seeing his face. He had the kind of smile that would make you smile instantly, and an infectious laugh too.

After he greeted everyone, he slowly walked over to me and said my name, "Misha." Then kissed me softly on the lips, squeezed me, and lifted me up off the ground. It felt like there was no one else in the room except him and I, in that moment. We stayed and socialized with his family for a while, then went to a hotel and made love in a way that showed how much we'd missed each other, time seemed to stop.

Mom came home from work one evening and said that her stomach was upset, but she thought it might have been from something she ate. The pain had become difficult for her to withstand, and so she contacted her doctor.

She went to the hospital where her doctor ran tests and took X-rays. He concluded that she had gallstones and would need surgery to remove them. She came home, packed a bag, and returned to the hospital for the surgery. I don't remember how long she stayed in hospital after surgery, perhaps a few days, before the doctor cleared her to return home.

All I remember at this point was she told us the surgery went well, and she felt much better. She didn't return to work during this time because she still needed to recover. A week went by and Mom noticed a yellowish fluid seeping through the incision line where she had the surgery. She waited a few days to see if it would clear up, and when it didn't, she called her doctor. He told her it sounded like an infection and advised her to return to the hospital so he could check it out. She prepared to leave the next day and told us she would be back later, then walked out the door. When I went inside my room, I saw a big manila envelope full of Mom's documents on my bed.

Mom's doctor did further tests and decided to admit her. I don't remember the reason why, other than she had an infection. She called home and told my brother Phil to bring more clothes and toiletries for her and gave instructions for us to continue our normal routine until she returned home.

She was at Brooklyn Hospital, the same hospital where I was born. I went to visit her the next day. She looked well, was talking and laughing with us. I waited until she and I were alone before I asked, "Mom, why did you leave the big manila envelope on my bed?"

"It's important paperwork that I didn't want to leave hidden without any of you knowing where to find it. There are things like bank account information, insurance policies, and your birth certificates. I'll take them back from you when I get home," she smiled at me. I felt proud that she entrusted me with something so important. I viewed it as a lesson in being responsible.

I visited her again two days later. She looked tired and seemed weak. She said she wasn't feeling that great, but I don't remember the reason why she felt tired and sick. We talked briefly before she drifted off to sleep.

I stayed a while longer watching her sleep, then kissed her on the cheek and left. I intended to come back the next day to visit her before going to see Will and his family. I was excited to spend more time with him. I was sure Mom's spirit and mood would be lifted when she saw my boyfriend all dressed up in his Air Force uniform. The thought made me smile as I walked out of the hospital.

I jumped on the train to meet Will at his brother's house in Queens. My intention was to get off the train when we got to the station for the hospital, but at the last minute, I thought it would be better to go visit Mom with my boyfriend after visiting with his family. When the train arrived at the station for the hospital, I didn't get off and just continued into Queens.

Will answered the door when I arrived at his brother's place. I went inside and greeted his brother- and sister-in-law. We sat at the table to eat dinner, and they asked how Mom was doing. I told them she had been tired lately and was hoping the doctor would find the reason for it.

"Would you mind going to visit Mom after we leave here?" I asked.

"Of course, I will go with you to visit Mom."

"She will be so happy to see you, especially in your uniform," I smiled.

He laughed, then the house phone rang, and Will got up to answer it. After about a minute, he came into the dining room and told me it was my brother Phil on the other line. Surprised, I went over to the kitchen and Will handed me the receiver, staying close to me.

"Hello…" Before I could say anything else, Phil began

speaking in a quivering voice and uttered the words, "Mommy just died, come home, honey."

From that moment, everything happened in slow motion. I stopped breathing, and the phone slipped out of my hands. I stood there, unable to move. Will picked the receiver off the floor and I heard him say to Phil that he was bringing me home now.

"Meesh, come here baby, I got you." He pulled me close to him and held me tightly. I felt a calm come over me, yet there were knots of fear in my stomach. Will's family came over, hugged me, and extended their condolences before we left to head back to Brooklyn. I don't remember anything about our train ride back to Brooklyn except that I was in a daze.

I was 15 years old when Mom died.

Liver cancer was her official cause of death. Liver cancer? She had surgery to remove gallstones. Where did liver cancer come from?

One of my mom's sisters worked at the hospital as a radiologist where Mom died and according to what Mom's doctor told her, Mom had liver cancer before the surgery to remove the gallstones, but having that surgery caused the cancer to spread quickly and end her life.

My brother Phil told me recently that my mom knew she had cancer yet refused to go through chemotherapy because it was against her Catholic faith. All these years passed, and I never knew that my mom not only knew she had cancer, but she also decided against treatment. Thirty years later, I'm still learning more about my mom, more than I ever knew when she was alive. Enigma.

When Will and I arrived at my house, I vaguely remember

what was going on. I remember seeing my brother Kevin and my sister Stephanie in the living room, but I don't remember specific conversations during that moment. I thought my dad was away related to his job as a longshoreman. However, I really don't know where he was at the time my mom died

Phil told me he had to gather information and paperwork together to give to two of my mom's sisters so they could take care of her funeral arrangements. Two days before Mom's funeral, one of Mom's sisters said that she had taken care of all arrangements and, if we needed anything, to let them know.

If we "needed anything," let them know!

I was 15, Kevin was 14, and Stephanie was 9. We most certainly would need much support, guidance, and continued cultivation with our upbringing. I don't remember seeing or speaking to any of my relatives immediately after Mom died.

My mom died two days before Will had to return to the Air Force. He said that he contacted his commander and explained the situation but was told that they would still consider him AWOL if he didn't return at his scheduled time. Will told me he was going to accept the penalty and stay for Mom's funeral. He ended up staying a week after we buried Mom.

Chapter Five

Funeral

June 23rd, 1980 was the day of Mom's funeral.

It was warm outside, not too hot or humid, and the sun shone brightly. I opened my closet and pulled out the dress I had bought a few days before to wear at Mom's funeral. It was a flowy, black chiffon dress with a light pink floral print. I completed the dress with light pink two-inch heeled sandals. Although my heart was heavy with grief, I didn't want to look like someone in mourning and intentionally chose an outfit that was bright and festive.

Mom would always turn on the radio in the morning to get the day started. We woke to the sounds of Classic Rock and R&B in the morning as we got ready for school. She was versatile in her taste of music: Elton John, the Beatles, Tom Jones, Dionne Warwick and Roberta Flack were some of her favorites. Mom also enjoyed classical music and played albums by Beethoven and Tchaikovsky. I felt embarrassed hearing the classical music coming from our window as I walked home from school. Black people don't listen to classical music, I thought. Why did Mom enjoy listening to this type of music? It was so strange to me.

As I got dressed and prepared for her funeral, I turned on the radio and instead of turning the dial to Classic Rock or an R&B station, I searched until I found the first classical sounds, closed my eyes and envisioned Mom sitting with her eyes closed, listening to this same score with such power to give her feelings of peace and calm. I opened my eyes and felt sorrow that she was gone, yet enjoyed reminiscing about her love for music and her specific appreciation for classical music. As I looked in the mirror, I smiled at how bright and cheery my outfit made me look. I turned off the radio, walked out of the house, and got into the limousine parked outside our door.

The church felt cold and dark, and it was filled with people I didn't know. I vaguely remember seeing Mom's three sisters and her mother as I approached the pulpit. I sat down and could hear the buzzing of people talking all around me as they waited for the sermon to start.

I looked at the pulpit and saw my mom's casket a few feet away. I could see a sideview of her upper body. I felt knots in my stomach and my heart beating a little faster. I didn't want my grief to overwhelm me and so I closed my eyes and put my head down.

I began praying and asking God to remove the knots from my stomach and help me get through this day. I stayed like this for a few minutes until I felt calm. I opened my eyes and lifted my head. I gazed over at Mom's coffin, and my mind drifted…

Mom was given away to foster parents by her mother when she was a little girl. Her biological mother, Ruth Bennett, was from Central America, Honduras, and her biological father was African American; his name was Charles Brown.

Her foster father was kind and loving, and her foster mother displayed love and affection when her foster father was present. However, as soon as he wasn't around, her foster mother became physically abusive. She would beat Mom in the head with a brush when she combed her hair and had Mom kneel on tall boiling pots that caused her knees to blister and bleed. Mom never shared any reasons for her mother giving her away or for her foster mother's abuse.

I met my mom's biological mother and maternal sister for the first time when I was six or seven years old. They were living in Boston at the time and came to visit us in Brooklyn. Shortly after meeting them, we also moved to Boston. I wondered if this was around the time Mom reconnected with her mother and decided to relocate us so that she could develop a stronger bond with her biological family. Mom also had a maternal brother; his name was Theodore. I don't remember meeting him when I was a small child, but we did meet when I was 13 years old, and I eventually became close with his wife and three children.

We stayed in Boston for only a year before Mom moved us back to Brooklyn. I don't know what happened with the relationship between Mom, her mother and sister, or the reason we stayed for only a short time in Boston. I don't remember seeing Mom's mother again until the day of her funeral.

Mom was a good-looking woman. Men paid her compliments and approached her often while we were out. During this time, we saw less and less of my dad. I'm not sure why, nor do I remember us asking Mom the reason for his infrequent visits. One day, she and I were leaving the supermarket in Brooklyn. There was a gold-colored Cadillac slowly driving alongside us as we walked with our groceries in the cart. The man inside the car was speaking to Mom. I heard Mom laugh and tell him her name. We stopped near the corner and he got out of the car; they stood there talking for a while, then he started taking our groceries and putting them in his car. He stooped down and asked, "What is your name?"

"My name is Misha," I said. He smiled and pinched my cheek. Mom told me to get into the car and he drove us home.

After that day, the same man, Mr. Leon, came to our house often and played with my brothers and me. He bought gifts, gave us money, and ate dinner with us too. He worked for New York City (NYC) Transit Authority as a dispatcher. Every time we played outside and saw him walking up the block, we ran towards him with excitement and joy. He was always smiling and seemed sincerely happy to see and be with us, too. He called me Meesh. I liked him a lot and felt comfortable and safe whenever he was around.

In 1970, Mom gave birth to my youngest sister, Stephanie. Her father was Mr. Leon. From the time my mom got pregnant until she gave birth, Mr. Leon came to our house after he got off work and spent most of his time with us. Mom was in love and very happy. Everything was going well, and our lives seemed stable. Little did we know, we were experiencing the quiet before a major storm.

One evening, a year later, I saw Mom take a bottle of what I thought was lotion but later found out from my brother Phil was a bottle of cleanser. She squirted it all over my infant sister's body. Phil grabbed a towel, lifted Steph and started wiping the solution off of her face and body. Mom put me and my brother Kevin in the bathroom and closed the door.

Smash. Boom. Shatter. Crunch! Glass breaking and pounding against the doors. The house shook like an earthquake and sounded like a tornado was ripping through it. Mom yelling and screaming in a voice that didn't sound like her. I kept my eyes closed and my arm around Kevin.

Suddenly, everything got quiet. I heard footsteps crunching against glass on the floor coming closer to the bathroom. A policeman opened the door, kneeling and smiling at me and my brother.

"What's your name?"

"I'm Misha and this is my brother Kevin," I answered.

He introduced himself and said he wanted to take us outside to let a nurse make sure that we were okay. We held his hand as he walked us out of the bathroom and through the kitchen and dining area. I remember seeing the dining room table flipped over and broken glass everywhere. The thick, heavy wooden door was off its hinges and had a huge dent in the center. I don't remember anything else about what happened after, except that Mom was diagnosed with having had a nervous breakdown. She was hospitalized for two months afterwards.

Phil remembered right before what happened, that Mom was playing a song by Aretha Franklin called, "Don't Play That Song for Me." She played it repeatedly, and it continued playing throughout her breakdown.

There may have been a few reasons for Mom's breakdown. First, she had bought our house a year prior and started working a third job. The other reason was that Mr. Leon changed his mind about coming to live with us permanently. Phil explained to me in later years that the woman he was living with at the time as a common-law spouse, threatened to take his pension and everything else he owned if he left. So, he told Mom that he couldn't be with us.

I believe all the abandonment, rejection, abuse, pain, heartbreak and still not finding the stability of a lasting relationship with someone she loved broke her completely.

As my mind returns to the scene of the funeral, I don't remember the eulogy or who gave it. I don't even remember going up to Mom's casket and seeing her one last time. It was all a blur. Will along with a few of my male relatives lifted Mom's casket up and placed it in the limousine. I rode to the cemetery with Will in his car. As we got closer to the cemetery, Will asked, "Are you okay?"

"Yes, I'm okay."

I was quiet the entire ride, thinking, Meesh, this situation is going to cause you to either sink or swim.

Will drove me back home and stayed with us for the rest of the day and into the night. He stayed in Brooklyn for a week before he had to return to his military base in Syracuse, New York.

I was grateful and comforted by having Will by my side throughout this difficult time. However, when it was time for him to leave, I couldn't help but feel that I was losing everyone I loved all at once. It's like my heart didn't have the chance to recover and prepare for the next loss.

Two days after we buried Mom, Stephanie's father took her away to live with him.

Chapter Six

Blood and Water

The day of Mom's burial was the last time I saw her mother and sisters. That was 41 years ago. Besides her maternal sister and brother, Mom had two paternal sisters: Adele and Beverly. I met them when I was 10 or 11 years old. The resemblance between the three was remarkable, especially between Mom and Adele. The two of them were a little darker in complexion than Beverly, yet all three had similar mannerisms, facial expressions, and laughs. I watched them together and thought, there's no denying they are sisters.

Beverly had two daughters and a son, and Adele was married with two daughters. Our families were very close. We spent the holidays and had many outings together. I loved them very much and believed that they loved Mom and us too, even though they had different mothers. I never saw or experienced ill treatment, or negative behavior towards us or Mom, until after we buried her.

After Mom's funeral, neither Beverly, Adele, or any of my other relatives offered help or opened their homes for me and my brother Kevin to live in. Initially, I was shocked and confused by the sudden shift in behavior, especially from my two aunts with whom we had a close and loving relationship. It didn't take long for me to accept that we had to figure it out for ourselves and make our own way.

Mom's mother and her maternal sister, Meryl, went back to Boston after the funeral without saying goodbye. To add insult to injury, a week after Mom's burial, we went to visit her at the cemetery and saw that she didn't have a headstone at her grave. "I thought Adele said they took care of all the funeral and burial arrangements for Mom," I said to Phil. I felt alternating waves of pain and anger as we stared quietly at the small peg sticking out from the dirt to mark Mom's gravesite.

It seemed everything that I thought was familiar and knew about my relatives became unrecognizable and foreign. What reason did they have for not honoring my mom's death with a headstone and for abandoning her children?

It took three decades and a casual conversation for the answers to be revealed. I was living abroad in 2005 and hadn't seen my siblings in ten years. In 2015, my nephew was graduating from high school and so I came home to attend his graduation and visit my siblings. During my stay, I went to see my sister-in-law, Cassy, and her mother. Cassy and my brother Kevin have been married for 27 years. Her mom, Gina, was always very good to Kevin and our families got along well.

Cassy and I greeted each other warmly, then sat, talked, and laughed about everything from the past up to the present. I was really enjoying my visit with her. Our conversation shifted to a gathering that she and Mom's sister Adele attended one evening. Adele came over and sat next to Cassy. According to Cassy, Adele had been drinking and angrily blurted out, "My father came home one day with Yvonne [Mom] and told me and Beverly that she was our sister! Beverly and I looked at each other with disdain upon hearing the news and when we were alone, we agreed we would never accept her as our real sister."

Cassy remained quiet and listened as Adele continued to express her anger about her dad fathering another child that wasn't from her mother.

It was one of those 'aha' moments when all the pieces of the puzzle fit, and the picture becomes clearer. Adele and Beverly feigned acceptance, love, and sincerity for Mom for all those years, which explained the lack of importance, honor, and dignity for Mom by their decision not to provide a headstone at her grave or security for her children. It also explained why Mom was given away to foster parents as a child. Her mother got pregnant with a man who was possibly married and already had children. Perhaps the shame and scandal that followed was too much for Mom's mother to bear.

It seemed impossible that anyone could endure such deep sorrow and pain as Mom did from the start to the end of her life. My heart grieved for a few seconds as I reflected on the information Cassy had shared with me. Yet, finally, I had concrete answers that allowed me to not only have complete closure about all that transpired around the time of Mom's death, but I felt compassion and forgiveness for them. This was the time God wanted me to have this information, and I was grateful to Him and Cassy for sharing it with me.

Phil and my dad had a meeting to devise a plan to help Kevin and I have stability and keep our family together. My dad still had a few years left at his job before he could retire and so his proposed plan was to get an apartment for the three of us to live together and he would visit periodically as his work permitted. Phil disagreed with Dad's plan because he believed we needed active and not passive parental guidance, which led to a fallout that ultimately left the relationship between them estranged.

Phil worked in the dietary department at a nursing home on the Upper East Side of Manhattan and was friends with a nurse, Lena, and a secretary, Glenda. The nurse sent flowers to Mom's funeral and expressed concern about the welfare of Kevin and me. The secretary also asked Phil what was happening with us. At the time, I was living with a good friend and her family in Brooklyn, and Kevin was living in a group home, also in Brooklyn.

Once Lena decided to take me, and Glenda to take Kevin, they spoke with and convinced Dad that we needed consistent parental guidance and structure that he couldn't provide at the time. They also worked with Phil to get Mom's pension paperwork together so that they could use the monthly check towards our needs while living with them.

My brother Kevin is not one to show or express emotions. He didn't cry at Mom's funeral. In fact, I don't ever remember seeing Kevin cry or become emotional. However, he did express his appreciation, gratitude, and the positive learning experience he gained during his time with Glenda.

I vaguely remember Phil and I meeting Lena at a restaurant so that she could inform me that I would be going to live with her and her son, Dorian. I liked Lena right away. Her presence felt friendly and comfortable. She had a light brown complexion, stood at about 5'4, and wore nice expensive clothes. Lena was in her late thirties at the time of our meeting.

"I just bought a house in Teaneck, New Jersey, and will be moving there in a few months. My son Dorian and I would love to have you live with us."

The thought of leaving Brooklyn was like getting a Brazilian wax, yet the idea of change and embarking upon the unknown was oddly thrilling, like my childhood days riding rollercoasters.

The first time I met Dorian was at their apartment in Harlem. "I wrote a poem for you," he said, and handed it to me. It was about birds in their nest singing in the air. Touched by the gesture, I hugged and thanked him. He was nine years old and already felt like my little brother.

I continued to stay at my girlfriend's house and go to school in Brooklyn during the week. On the weekends, I stayed with Lena and Dorian at their apartment in Harlem. They picked me up early Saturday morning, and we had brunch at Sylvia's, a Harlem landmark restaurant, famous for delicious Southern food. The salmon cakes and biscuits were to die for.

Lena took me shopping for clothes, shoes, and anything else I needed or wanted. The two months I spent with her and Dorian made me feel safe, cared for, and comfortable. Despite my sense of comfort and acceptance about moving to Teaneck, as the time approached for us to leave Harlem, my world was completely turned upside down, coming apart strand by strand. My mother had just died suddenly. None of my blood relatives wanted to take us. My siblings and I were abruptly uprooted and separated from each other, and now I was to live with complete strangers in an environment totally unfamiliar to me.

I reflected on all this a few days before the move, cried myself to sleep and had a dream…

I saw myself in a bright house with white walls all around and I was standing at the top of the stairs looking at a bunch of colorful balloons covering the front door. The image of the colorful balloons made me feel calm, and I slept peacefully the rest of the night, feeling less apprehensive about moving to Teaneck.

A few weeks after we moved into the house in Teaneck, I was upstairs and heard the doorbell ring. I walked over to the top of the stairs, looked towards the front door, and saw a man in a delivery uniform hand Lena a bunch of big colorful balloons before asking that she sign her name on the clipboard he held.

"Look Misha, aren't the balloons beautiful!"

"Congratulations on the new house!" the card read from her co-workers.

It was my dream!

Chapter Seven

Transitions

I moved to a suburb that felt like a foreign country six months after Mom's burial. My new address was 161 Evergreen Place, Teaneck, New Jersey. Our yellow single-family house sat on a hill surrounded by tall, green, beautiful trees, cut grass and birds singing. The house had three bedrooms, two bathrooms, a breakfast nook, dining room, a basement, and two entrances. It was a cute little house that had the space to accommodate the three of us comfortably. I was glad to have my own room and privacy; it helped with my transition from Brooklyn.

At the bottom of the hill was Milton A. Votee Park, which featured an in-ground pool, wooded walking trails, a playground, and a tennis court. The sky was blue and clear. The air was fresh and clean during the day, but at night the smell of skunk often seeped through the screened windows. I used to think raccoons were cute until I saw one up close.

One night, we drove up the driveway to the garage at the back of the house and there it was, rummaging through our recycle bin. The headlights shined on it, but the raccoon turned, looked at us, and continued rummaging.

"He's not even afraid," I said to Lena and Dorian. We sat in the car for a few minutes, watching him. I was creeped out by how human his hands and nails looked. Lena laughed at my reaction.

Growing up in the city, I'd never seen wildlife roam freely outside of a zoo. I wondered what other wildlife I might encounter: a bear, snake, or wolf? I started to like almost everything about my new environment, except wildlife and shoveling snow.

Teaneck was a small, charming township that reminded me of a few other small towns with big personalities like those featured in a Stephen King novel. Cedar Lane was a main shopping area with a variety of restaurants, novelty stores, and a small cinema. Pizza, burgers at the diner, and an old-fashioned ice cream shop were some of my favorite things.

At first, I welcomed the novelty of living in such a scenic, quiet environment. I enjoyed having close access to the park and often jogged along the trails. The New Jersey Transit bus operations provided service between New York and New Jersey, and the bus stopped at the bottom of the hill, which made it convenient for me to get to the city. There was a small laundromat, a dry cleaner, deli, and nightclub near our house. Sometimes we spent weekends shopping at the malls near Teaneck, and other times went to Manhattan for brunch.

Thoughts of Will weighed heavily on my heart. The last time I saw him was a few months after mom died and before I moved to Teaneck. I visited him at his barracks in Syracuse, NY. After that, he was sent somewhere overseas, and we lost contact.

Lena was a jazz enthusiast and frequently went to Greenwich Village to listen to concerts in the city. I thought jazz music was for bored, old people. I couldn't understand why anyone wasted time listening to loud noises from instruments without lyrics.

"Young people listen to jazz, and some are jazz musicians," said Lena. "Listen to this young, up-and-coming saxophone player, Brennan Marshall."

"I'm not listening to that noise," I mumbled and rolled my eyes. Lena showed me Brennan's album cover. I glanced at his picture, then did a double take.

"Hahaha, you should see your face, Misha. He's handsome, isn't he?"

"This guy is a jazz musician, plays the saxophone, and is around my age?" I asked.

I had no idea what a jazz musician looked like, but I was certain they didn't look like Brennan. It was enough to pique my curiosity about jazz music. That evening, I listened to Brennan's album, and to my surprise, the sounds of the instruments playing together in harmony were quite soothing to my soul. I laid on my bed with my eyes closed, listening attentively, and experienced different emotions arise from each instrument. There was something very seductive and romantic about the sound of the saxophone. It drew me in. I felt compelled to explore more about this music called jazz and the reason someone in my generation bothered to center his life around it.

I started going to the Village and the Cultural Jazz Center with Lena to listen to music by different artists. The artists were good, but my favorite thing to do was to order chicken and waffles at 2 AM, the best eats in Harlem. The clubs in Greenwich Village had a certain vibe that instantly energized you. A cloud of smoke and the noise from the band rose to a crescendo the moment you entered. Lena knew a lot of people in both places and even had a few friends who were professional jazz musicians, too.

One weekend, she asked me if I wanted to go with her to see a famous drummer and piano player in the Village.

"Hmmm, I'm feeling lazy and don't feel like getting dressed," I said

"Brennan will be playing in the band too."

"Are you serious?"

"Yes, very serious, here's the flyer."

I saw Brennan's name on the flyer and told Lena not to leave me. All I heard was laughter as I ran up the stairs. I laughed at myself too, the things we do when the opposite sex is involved. I was dressed and ready to go in 20 minutes. During our drive into the city, I started daydreaming about what I'd say to Brennan if I were able to speak to him. I wondered how different I would feel seeing and listening to his music live.

My stomach churned as we got closer. We found a parking spot nearby and walked inside, then took the elevator two flights up where the doors opened to a large banquet hall.

"I thought we were going to a club, Lena."

"The musicians are playing for a charity organization and they decided to host the event here," she said.

Lena, her two girlfriends, and I sat at a table near the stage. I scanned the hall in search of Brennan. All at once, the musicians came out from behind a curtain onto the stage. One man sat down at the piano; another man picked up the bass. The lead of the band was the drummer, and Brennan placed his saxophone across his chest.

Immediately, they began playing, and I observed the facial

expressions and body language of each musician. Brennan had a very cool and relaxed demeanor in the way he stood and played. He was tall, very good-looking, and wore his clothes well. I was starstruck.

When the first set was finished, the musicians walked off the stage and mingled with the audience. I saw someone speaking to Brennan and waited for an opportunity to speak to him myself. As soon as the opportunity presented itself, I calmly approached him.

"Hi, I'm Misha."

"Hi Misha, I'm Brennan," he extended his hand to shake mine.

"Nice to meet you, Brennan. I sent a letter to you a few weeks ago."

"Oh really? I never received it. Where did you send it?"

"I sent it to an address listed on your album cover."

"I'm sorry I didn't get it. What did your letter say?"

I explained how I never listened to jazz music until his album and it not only changed the way I viewed jazz but how much I enjoyed it.

"Wow, I'm glad to hear that you're learning about an important part of our cultural history and enjoying it, too."

I asked Brennan if he minded signing his autograph on the album liner.

I handed it to him, and he wrote, "To Misha, keep learning and listening to the music and thank you for the letter, Brennan."

Lena and her friends walked over to us. I introduced them to Brennan, then Lena said they were ready to leave. I turned to Brennan and thanked him for signing the album liner.

We all started walking toward the elevator. Brennan and I trailed behind them, continuing to talk. Once we reached the elevator, the doors opened, and we walked inside.

"It was nice meeting you all," said Brennan. He looked at me, smiled, and leaned his body inside the elevator, kissed me on the cheek, and the doors closed. Stunned, I looked at Lena and her friends. You could hear a pin drop in the elevator. Then, in unison, they teased me. "Oh boy! Brennan kissed Misha, muah, muah muah, hehe, haha." I don't remember getting in the car, where we went afterward, or what time we got home. I replayed every detail of that evening in my mind and savored the memory.

Brennan is a very famous jazz musician today. I continued to go see him at the clubs whenever he played in New York City and from those encounters, we formed a friendship. One evening, after work, I decided to stop by Radio City Music Hall. Brennan was performing there with a famous mainstream artist who wasn't a jazz musician. The collaboration between the two, mainstream and jazz, proved to be hugely successful and sold many albums. I was proud of Brennan for taking a chance and showing his versatility and skill as a sax player, not just a jazz musician.

The backdoor was barricaded by police, and tons of people stood there hoping to get a glimpse of artists and celebrities. I wrote a short note asking Brennan to come outside, then went over to a policeman behind the barricade. "Excuse me officer, would you mind going inside and giving this note to Brennan. He's a friend."

"You're a friend of Brennan Marshall?" he smirked.

"Yes, I really do know him. Please, officer, give him the note."

Reluctantly, the officer went inside. About five minutes later, he came back outside, and Brennan was behind him. He asked the officer where I was, and the officer pointed in my direction. As soon as Brennan saw me, he smiled and motioned for me to come. The officer came over to remove the barricade for me to come inside. "You really do know Brennan," he smiled.

"I told you."

Brennan and I embraced, then I followed him up the stairs. "I'm going to introduce you to a few people."

"Okay," I smiled. He opened the door, and we were backstage. We started to walk towards where the people had gathered when I saw the artist Sting coming towards Brennan and me.

Brennan introduced us.

"Hello, Misha."

I couldn't believe I was in front of Sting. Brennan asked him if he was leaving and he said he was going out for a while but would return shortly. Then he turned to me, "Nice meeting you, Misha."

As we reached the main area, Brennan introduced me to Jennifer Beals and I also got a glimpse of Mick Jagger as we mingled around a bit.

"I have one more person for you to meet." We walked through more people and went into a small lounge area. A very pregnant woman stood up and smiled. Brennan introduced her as his fiancé. I smiled as my heart sank and extended my hand to shake hers. I congratulated her on the pregnancy and engagement, then asked Brennan to walk me out.

When we got to the stairwell, I asked him when the engagement happened.

"When she got pregnant," he responded, then he sat on the steps. We were quiet for a few seconds, then I asked him if he was happy. He said he was, but his face didn't appear to be. We chatted for a few more minutes, and I thanked him for an exciting evening. He laughed. As we got to the bottom of the steps and walked out the back door, we faced each other and, once again, embraced. "You gotta come see the baby."

I smiled, "Of course I will. Goodnight Bren."

"Good night, Misha."

I walked over to a beautiful fountain located diagonally across from Radio City Music Hall and sat there for a few minutes, crying. Why am I crying? I wondered. Brennan and I are friends. I hadn't given much thought to Brennan and I becoming more than friends until that night. There was no chance of that ever happening now, and a part of me felt sad about that reality. I pulled myself together and walked to Port of Authority and caught the bus back to New Jersey.

Less than a year later, Brennan and his wife had a son, Ross. I visited them at their house in Brooklyn and held Ross. At the time, I was going through a transition of a spiritual nature and knew I wouldn't see Brennan after that day. It was the last time we saw each other in person.

As the summer was coming to an end, I prepared to attend high school in Brooklyn. I knew it would be a long commute, but I needed a connection to what I still considered home. Lena tried to convince me to attend Teaneck High School and took me there to explore all they had to offer. I vaguely remember the details of our visit, but when we arrived on the campus, I do remember how impressed I was by the huge campus situated on a hill with its beautiful and impeccable landscape.

Teaneck High School appeared to be the perfect place to learn and study. Yet I also remember seeing a few kids getting out of expensive cars and instinctively felt that this environment of wealthy, entitled kids wasn't for me. I was a city girl at heart, a die-hard Brooklyn native to the core, and in my mind, I had already been stripped of so many people and things near and dear to me. Commuting to my high school in Brooklyn was the sole option for me. That high school was William H. Maxwell, an all-girls vocational school at the time, located on Pennsylvania Ave in the East New York section of Brooklyn.

I caught the bus at the bottom of the hill every morning at 6 AM. The ride from Teaneck to Port Authority in Midtown Manhattan took between 45 and 60 minutes, depending on traffic. I took two trains from there and arrived at school between 7:30 to 7:45 AM. I enjoyed the commute. Looking out the window at the various scenes going through New Jersey and watched the transition as we approached the city. It felt in many ways therapeutic to me. I also got a chance to eat breakfast, complete unfinished homework, and sometimes, strike up a conversation with a commuter.

Lena also commuted. She was an administrator at a hospital in New York and so she drove into the city daily, too. Many times, I rode into the city with her, then caught the trains to school. It was a pleasant routine that I looked forward to during the week. Wintertime was a little challenging; the bitter cold and heavy snowstorms weren't fun at all. Dorian and I also had to shovel snow from the driveway and from the walkway, a task that was equally no fun. In fact, it was the worst chore I could have been assigned, especially since I never had to do that when living in Brooklyn.

After about six months of commuting to school and living in Teaneck, I started working a part-time job as a call center representative in a town not far from Teaneck. I worked some weekends for a few hours. I met a few people that became friends. Two of those friends lived in Teaneck too: Violet and Melissa were their names. Melissa lived around the corner from me and Violet about a five-minute drive away. Violet and I became closer and hung out more. I also started dating around this time.

One Saturday morning I was at the laundromat and this tall, handsome, medium brown complexioned guy came over and introduced himself to me. His name was Kurt, and he was on leave from the Marine Corps to visit his family.

I gave him my number, and we had a nice lunch date a week later. He called me early one morning and asked if I wanted to go to the recreational center with him to watch a basketball competition, he was playing in. I accepted his invite, and he said he would pick me up at my house.

A few hours later, I heard the doorbell ring. I was upstairs combing my hair when Lena shouted, "Misha, Kurt is here!"

"Okay, I'll be right down."

After ten minutes, I came down the stairs and walked towards the side entrance where Lena and Kurt were waiting. I smiled at Kurt, but he looked terrified. I noticed an ace bandage wrapped around his right hand up to his thumb.

"What happened to your hand, Kurt?"

"I'll tell you about it in the car," he abruptly replied. Without saying goodbye to Lena, he practically ran out the door.

When I got into Kurt's car he asked, "What's up with your Mom?" his face flushed. I turned my whole body towards him, "What do you mean?"

"Your Mom came close to me and lifted up my injured hand and asked, 'What happened, baby?' Then she started kissing my hand! I snatched my hand away and said, 'What are you doing?' That's when you came down the stairs."

After a short pause, I blurted out, "She's not my real mother."

"She's not your real mother!"

"No, she's not even a blood relative. My Mom died, and I came to live with her."

Kurt slumped back in his seat. "I'm sorry that you lost your Mom, Misha."

"Me too, thanks. Are you ready to go win this basketball competition?"

"Hell, yeah," he smiled confidently, and we drove off.

There were two additional incidents like the one that occurred with other male friends, each of them informing me in detail about inappropriate advances made towards them when they came to our house to pick me up for a date. What would make a mother commit an act of betrayal to this degree, jeopardizing the close bond between mother and daughter?

These incidents destroyed my trust and caused me to want to get far away. It was time to leave Lena's house and make my own way. Shortly after the last incident, I went to Lena and asked her to sign me out of high school so that I could attend Job Corps. Puzzled, she asked, "Why do you want to leave school for Job Corps?"

"I want to get a GED and learn a skill so that I can get a job and live on my own."

At this point, I hadn't confronted Lena about the incidents with my male friends.

"Well, I don't think it's the best decision to leave school at 16 years old."

"I want to leave, so please sign me out of school."

She and I went back and forth about this issue. Finally, she said she would get more information about Job Corps and then we could discuss it after.

She and I met with a Job Corps recruitment counselor in Brooklyn and by the time our meeting was over, Lena was satisfied with all the information the counselor provided about the program and safety. Lena agreed to sign me out but had one last requirement for me to fulfill beforehand. I had to maintain a B grade in every subject for the final quarter of my report card. I was determined to meet her requirement and spent the next three months laser-focused on every subject at school.

By the end of the final quarter, I received all B's and a few B pluses. Oh, happy day. I'm out of here! When Lena saw my grades, she laughed, "You really do want to get out of here!"

"Yes, I really do."

"A deal is a deal, you got it, Misha. I'll sign you out of school."

I relaxed instantly and started preparing for life on my own at Job Corp.

Chapter Eight

Job Corps

After a long 12-hour bus ride, I arrived at Cassadaga Job Corps Center in Upstate New York. It was the middle of August and the weather was nice. The Greyhound bus left from the Port Authority in Midtown Manhattan at midnight. I slept most of the trip. When I opened my eyes and looked out of the window, I saw a breathtaking view of rolling hills, beautiful lakes, and a variety of trees.

Dunkirk and Fredonia were the last two station stops we made before entering the town of Cassadaga. Five people got off at the Cassadaga bus station, including me. I got my bags from the bus and walked into the station where two smiling African American women greeted the five of us. One woman pulled out a sheet of paper and began calling our names. They introduced themselves as our guidance counselors from the Job Corps Center.

It was a short ride from the bus station to the center. We came to check-in at the gate. Two security guards were inside a little hut. The police officers greeted us and raised the poles for us to enter. The counselors asked us to follow them for a quick tour of the campus. The cafeteria, most of the vocational training programs, and the male dormitory were near the right side of the main building. As we walked towards the left side, I saw a steep hill with a huge building sitting at the top. That building was the female dormitory.

"I know you all are exhausted from the trip, so we won't walk to the top of the hill today," Ms Simmons smiled. Midway up, Ms. White pointed to a building on the right and informed us that that was the healthcare training program.

Once at the top of the hill, I gasped. We had a 360-degree panoramic view of Chautauqua County. I walked over to the edge of the hill, looked down, and saw amongst all the greenery, wooded forests, and lakes, several small towns. The view was magnificent, and I noticed a quiet stillness in the air that made me feel relaxed and at peace with my decision to be there.

The lobby was a very large, open area that was set up like a recreation room. It had a few sofas, a ping-pong table, and a separate dining area. There was an east and west side to the dorm. The counselors mentioned that the dorm was once a tuberculosis hospital, which explained the size and divisions inside.

We went up the stairs to the east side of the dorm, which the counselor said housed four, six, and eight girls in a room. I arrived at a room that had three other girls, with four twin-sized mattresses, four desks and chairs, and plenty of closet space. There were two windows on opposite sides of the room.

"Misha, this is your room. You ladies introduce yourselves and make Misha feel comfortable. There's a good chance you'll move to a two-room in a few months depending on availability and good behavior," said Ms. Simmons. It didn't bother me being in a room with three other girls. I was excited to be there. What I saw left a good impression on me. I felt like I belonged.

The three girls and I introduced ourselves and talked for a long time about everything. We each came from different backgrounds, situations, and had extraordinary stories, yet we all seemed to be alike in many ways. I spent the rest of the time unpacking my clothes and settling into my new world.

Our day started at six o'clock. I showered, got dressed, made my bed (a dorm rule and requirement), and headed down the hill to the cafeteria. Academic training started at eight until lunchtime at noon. At one o'clock we went to vocational training, which lasted until five. I chose the Certified Nursing Assistant program. The instructor was a great teacher, caring and extremely funny. Her name was Ms. T. We ate dinner around six o'clock and a curfew was in place at nine.

We were free to do what we wanted during those hours after dinner and before curfew. Many of the students were couples, even though boys and girls were not allowed to enter each other's dormitories. If you were caught, you could be sent home. It was a strict rule.

I settled into the daily routine and was learning more about the other students on campus. Most students were from the New York/New Jersey area and everyone seemed to be addressed by their nicknames: Killer, Slim, Peaches, Grandma, Lil' Bit, just to name a few. They even gave me a nickname, (it was the guys, of course): Hairy Canary. Why? The name itself should be obvious. I had a lot of hair on my head, arms, and legs. I wasn't crazy about the name, but it was the truth and so I answered to it. A sense of community developed as we became more familiar with one another, and I was completely comfortable with the assortment of characters.

There was much talk among my community about liquor runs and mediums that lived in a neighboring town called Lily Dale. A few of the older students in our dorm told us that if we ever wanted to get a "reading" by a medium, we could go to Lily Dale for the day.

"What is a reading? And who is a medium?" I asked.

"A medium is someone who can tell you what will happen in the future and also communicate with spirits," one student said in a low voice. "It's called a reading."

It sounded creepy and intriguing at the same time.

"Liquor runs are when students sneak off campus to a nearby town to buy alcohol. It's very risky because security patrols the entire campus 24-hours a day, all day, and on weekends too. If you're caught, you'll be expelled and sent home immediately."

I was curious about the liquor run. A wild side of me was drawn to taking that risk.

"When is the next run?" I asked.

"Leshawn on the West Side is planning to make a run on Saturday."

The next day, I spoke with Leshawn and asked her if I could go with her on the run.

"Aren't you new here?"

"Yeah, I am."

"You know what can happen if we get caught?"

I nodded.

"As long as you know, the risk is on you."

"Got it. So tell me what I need to know?"

The sound of the loudspeaker came on, "Attention ladies, please report to the recreational area now for an emergency meeting."

"We'll talk later," Leshawn got up and I followed.

I hardly slept on Friday night anticipating my first liquor run. When I woke up and looked out the window, all I saw was a sheet of white covering everything. Ten to 12 inches of snow had fallen, and it was just nine o'clock. I walked over to Lashawn's room, knocked on the door, and before anyone answered, I saw Leshawn coming up the stairs.

"Hey, I was coming to ask you if we were still on for today?"

"Of course, a little snow ain't going to stop a run."

It was music to my ears.

"Make sure you layer your clothes and I hope you have snow boots!" Leshawn laughed.

"I have a whole ski suit and yeah, I have snow boots too."

"Good. Listen Misha, we're going sledding. We'll slide down the hill a few times as a cover, then run into the woods with the sleds."

"Do you know your way there and back very well, Leshawn?"

"Yes, relax, Misha, I've done this many times. Are you scared?"

"No, I'm not scared. I just don't want to be lost in the woods during a snowstorm."

"Hahahah, just keep up with me and you'll be fine."

Leshawn shoved a shortlist of orders from her roommates in her pocket and we grabbed the sleds from the recreation room and headed outside. It was lightly snowing, and the ground was covered with layers of snow. We walked towards the back of the dorm, placed the sleds a few inches away from each other, sat down, and held on to the straps in front of the sled.

"Ready?" she asked.

"Let's do it!"

Down we slid to the bottom of the hill. It was so much fun. I felt my adrenaline pumping in a good way.

"Okay, we're going to do it two more times."

I grabbed the straps and pulled the sled up the hill. On the third slide down, we saw a police car patrolling our area. Once we got to the bottom, Leshawn said we should slide down one more time to give us time for the police guards to finish patrolling the area near the woods.

The fourth time down the hill, the police were out of sight and we started running towards the woods, pulling the sleds behind us. We slowed our run to a light jog as we got deeper into the woods. I stayed right beside Leshawn, keeping up with her pace.

I asked why we had to take the sleds?

"It would look suspicious if we left them behind. Besides, it will help carry the liquor."

Hmmm, that made a lot of sense. My heart was thumping out of my chest from running and from fear that a snowman with a chainsaw would jump out from a tree unexpectedly. Leshawn said cutting through the woods was a shortcut into town to the liquor store. It took us about 20 minutes to jog our way there.

I saw an opening and across the street was the liquor store, along with a few other stores clustered next to each other. We left the sleds in the woods and I went to the back of the store and got a few cases of Heineken beer while Leshawn read her list to the clerk. She paid for everything and the clerk bagged all the liquor. We walked out of the store with the heavy bags and back into the woods.

We evenly distributed the weight of the alcohol on both sleds and began walking back toward the center. The snow was coming down heavier and we couldn't run or jog because of the weight on the sleds. I felt like I was competing on a gladiator show tugging the beer on the sled. It was very heavy.

We stopped and rested a few times, which doubled the time it took to return. Finally, I could see the bottom of the hill.

"How are we going to lug these cases of beer up the hill?" I asked.

"Wait here, I'm going to find some of the guys to help us." She ran down the hill to the guys' dorm and came back with Dre and Slim.

"What? Hairy-Canary went on a run!"

"Blah, blah, blah, Slim, can we go now!" I replied

Slim always joked around with everyone. He was very tall and slender, hence the nickname Slim. Dre had a quiet, shy demeanor. "You okay, Misha?"

"I'm good, Dre, just hungry right about now."

Slim and Dre held the straps on the sled and peeped out from the woods, then started running up the hill. Exhausted, Leshawn and I leisurely walked up the hill. Slim and Dre placed the sleds inside the dorm's entryway. Leshawn pulled out a six-pack of beer and gave it to them.

"Thank you, my brothers!" Slim grinned, turned away, and started walking down the hill.

Leshawn went inside the dorm and Dre asked me if I was dating anyone on campus.

"No, why do you ask?"

He walked a few steps away from me, then turned around

smiling. "Pretty girls don't go on runs!" then quickly ran down the hill. I watched him dart down the hill until he was out of sight and I walked inside the dorm, straight to my room.

Shortly after this encounter, Dre and I started dating. Every day he waited for me to get out of class, then walked me to my dorm. He was a great boyfriend who treated me like a princess. He was also the leader of a drug operation at the center. How did I know? He ordered dinner from a restaurant off-center and invited me to join him in his room. There was a knock on the door and a police officer greeted Dre and handed him the food. Right after we ate, he pulled out a boxed Pepperidge Farm chocolate cake.

"Dessert!" was my reaction.

Dre looked at me from across the table with a serious face. "Before we eat the cake, there's something I want to share with you that no one in this center knows about except one person. It's a big secret, Misha, and I'm trusting you not to tell anyone."

"Of course, Dre, you can trust me."

He slowly opened the box and pulled out the cake. Half of the cake was gone and replaced with a tightly rolled, large ziplock bag. He picked up the bag, opened it, and removed a handful of marijuana.

"This is how the drugs got in and you're the source!" I thought this was genius. Dre's quiet and shy disposition was the perfect cover to eliminate him from ever being a suspect.

"Do you want to break up with me?"

I laughed. "Of course not, you're a good guy and this doesn't change anything." I kept his secret for many years. In fact, this is the first time I've ever told anyone.

Leshawn left a whole case of beer on my bed, and I was alone in the room. I took a long, hot shower, put on my warm pajamas, grabbed a Heineken, and sat on the windowsill looking at the snow falling quietly. As I stared out into the forest, two gray deer came out from the woods. Oh, wow. Gray deer! I had never seen them before, and they were beautiful.

It warmed my heart to see deer just a few feet away from my window. I couldn't stop smiling as I observed their beauty, the stark snow in the background against their lovely shade of gray. Just then, someone in the dorm turned up the volume from a radio as "Quiet Storm" by Smokey Robinson began to play. The dorm had perfect acoustics to hear the wind blowing and whistling at the beginning of the song.

Soft and warm, a quiet storm, quiet as when flowers talk at break of dawn, break of dawn... I closed my eyes and visualized Smokey's brilliant lyrics. What a great song and perfect timing. I slowly opened my eyes and continued to enjoy the sights and sounds of a quiet storm all around me.

I was learning about myself and others at Job Corps and growing with each new experience. I wasn't afraid or homesick. Our classes prepared us well to pass the GED exam. The Shoemakers were a husband-and-wife team, and they taught all academic subjects. They lived in Lily Dale, as did other faculty members at the center. Everyone seemed calm and friendly, which made it easy to approach them or ask questions.

I asked my roommate, Pam, about Lily Dale. She knew nothing about it, but suggested we ask our dorm leader, Lil Bit, who had lived at the center longer than any other student.

Lil Bit was 5'2 and very petite. She always had a serious look on her face.

"Lily Dale is a place the two of you should visit. Most people living there talk with spirits."

My heart started to beat faster. "You mean they talk to spirits?" Lil Bit smirked, "It's possible to talk with spirits, there are spirits all around us." Fear came over my body and something didn't feel right about what she was saying.

"Have you guys ever played with the Ouija board before?"

I had never heard of it.

Pam shouted, "That game is evil!"

Lil Bit burst out in laughter. "It's not evil. Sometimes spirits appear and help answer questions people have about their deceased loved ones." She told us if we didn't want to play with the Ouija board, then we should go sit with a medium in Lily Dale and hear what they have to say. "They can tell you about things that will happen in the future."

"So, they're fortunetellers?"

"Not exactly. They don't use a crystal ball or dress like a gypsy. Info just comes to them during your conversation."

The conversation about these mediums was scary, yet fascinating. I was into horoscopes and read about the positions of planets and how one's birth makes up an astrological chart, but Ouija boards and mediums were on a whole different level.

Pam and I walked away from Lil Bit and without a word, we agreed that playing with the Ouija board was out of the question. Later that evening, we returned to the dorm and found a group of girls in the middle of the recreation room in a circle around the Ouija board with Lil Bit.

I moved into a two-person room about three or four months later and shared my room with a girl named Lisa. Everyone called her Grandma because she was very caring and nurturing. She was from New Jersey and we instantly connected and became good friends.

One day, I came back to the room after class and Lisa had put her desk in the center of our room and the Ouija board on top of the table.

"What the f—, Lisa!"

"Meesh, listen, I know you don't like this board game, but I've heard some girls say it gives you real answers to questions you ask."

"Lisa, this game is a hoax. I don't believe the disk moves on its own."

"I have a question I want to ask, and it has nothing to do with dead people. Meesh, please, play it with me just for one question."

Rolling my eyes, I said, "Okay, Lisa, one question, then you'll see for yourself that it's not real."

She closed the window curtains and turned off the lights.

"Oh boy, you're really getting into this," I chuckled.

"C'mon, be serious so it can work."

I was not serious about this game at all. We sat opposite of each other and placed our fingertips on the white disk.

"Ouija board, can I ask you a question?"

After 30 seconds, the disk moved to the word yes. I thought she made the disk move, just like those girls from before.

"Ouija board, am I pregnant now?"

I looked up at her, surprised. She shrugged her shoulders. Within a few seconds the disk slowly moved to the word "no".

"See, Misha, it does answer questions."

"Okay, now I'll ask a question. Ouija board, am I pregnant?" I knew I wasn't, but I was trying to make a point that this game was fake. The disk didn't move immediately. I smirked, thinking to myself, I knew this game was bullsh—.

I felt a cool breeze over my hands and the disk started moving even more slowly than before. I looked at the window to see if it was open at all to explain the breeze I felt on my hand, but the windows were closed, and the curtains hadn't moved.

"Lisa, stop playing. Are you moving the disk?"

In a crackled voice, she said, "No, Meesh, I'm not moving it at all."

My fight-or-flight response kicked in quickly, and I held my breath to hear or see anything that was moving the disk.

"Lisa, let's lift our fingers off the disk."

As we did it, we saw the disk moving by itself and watched it glide and land on the word "yes". Terrified, I told Lisa to turn on the lights as I slumped back into my seat.

We remained silent for a minute, looking at the board. The damn disk was moving on its own.

"WTF, Lisa!"

"I felt a presence near my hands that scared the sh— out of me, Misha!"

"Yeah, I felt a cool breeze or like the wind blowing over my hands. This isn't normal and I'm not pregnant!"

"I'm not sure if I am or not. That's why I wanted to ask it. I'll go to the infirmary tomorrow and take a blood test to confirm that I'm not," said Lisa.

"I don't think I am either, but I'll go with you and get tested, too. The moving disk messed my head up and don't ask me to play this game with you again."

"I'm done with that game, too. Let's get something to eat."

We went downstairs and ordered some food from a local restaurant. Thirty minutes later, we came back to the room and when we opened the door, the room was freezing. I saw the curtain blowing outside the window.

"Did you open the window before we left the room, Lisa?"

"You know I didn't open any window. We left together."

We looked at each other, grabbed our food, and hauled our asses out of there. We slept in the recreation room that night in fear that the spirit who moved the disk might return while we slept. It was one of the most uncomfortable and inexplicable moments in my life. The most troubling part of the whole experience occurred a few days later, when my pregnancy results were negative and Lisa's results were positive.

The next day, I went to visit my first roommate, Pam, and shared my story with her.

"I'm speechless, Misha."

"You and I both, Pam. The fact that we both asked it if we were pregnant, and one of us is, has me curious about visiting a medium in Lily Dale. I want to understand more about this supernatural stuff. I don't know what will happen in Lily Dale, but I want to see and have the experience of a medium for myself. Would you mind going with me?"

"I don't mind at all. I'm curious. When do you want to go?"

"I'll ask Mrs. Shoemaker if she can arrange a day."

Mrs. Shoemaker taught math and social studies and recommended a good friend who was a medium.

Pam and I arranged a round-trip ride with a taxi service for our

Saturday meeting. It was a 15-minute drive from the center to get there. Lily Dale felt eerily quiet and still, like something was about to happen. We got out of the taxi and knocked on the lady's door. A slender, medium height, pleasant woman answered and invited us inside. She introduced herself and explained that she would speak with us individually and asked who wanted to go first.

Eager and anxious, I volunteered to go first. She smiled and asked Pam to wait in an adjoining room. She returned to the living room and sat in a chair facing me.

"Before we get started, please know, whatever we discuss today may not happen right away. Just try to remember what we've spoken about, as it may come up later or at another time."

"Okay, I understand."

"Have you or someone close to you lost a child?"

"No, I've never been pregnant."

"I see a child that died very young."

"My mom lost her firstborn child when he was a little boy."

"Perhaps that's who I'm seeing. Do you know someone named Angela? She has a faint stain on one of her front teeth?"

"No, I don't know anyone by that name."

"This person is deceitful and will betray you in some way. Just remember that we spoke about it."

"How do you know these things?"

"It just comes to me," she smiled.

It appeared that she was listening to something or someone as she asked me a question or made a statement. She asked me about my friend Greg and said he would eventually become a successful songwriter. At the time, he was just starting out writing songs.

I don't remember anything else she asked me or what she told Pam that day. However, eleven years later I was married, got pregnant, and had an ectopic pregnancy after two and a half months. I believe I encountered at least two Angelas that fit the medium's description along my journey. I kept them at arm's length.

My curiosity at 16 years old was satisfied, and I didn't feel the need to further explicate matters of the supernatural or delve deeper into knowledge about unseen or hidden affairs. Not everything should be sought after, nor is it necessary to have the answers to all things. Some knowledge is kept hidden for a reason, and I'm good with that.

It was just under a year later when I took the GED exam and passed it on the first try, scoring 60 points above the passing score. I also received my Nursing Assistant Certification. The guidance counsellors called me and five other students to their office to inform us that we were offered scholarships to our choice of college in Vermont or Southern California. I was very excited and chose to go to Southern Vermont College.

A week before we prepared to leave, the guidance counsellors scheduled another meeting with us to relay that the US Dept of Labor had unexpected budget cuts and that they had to rescind our scholarships for college. We were all devastated. I called Lena and told her about the change. She was very angry and said she was going to make some calls. Two days later, Ms. Simmons and Ms. White asked me and the other five students to come to their office.

"Misha, I don't know who your mom is or knows, but we just got a call from a representative at the Department of Labor and they decided to give you students the scholarships."

We all jumped up and down and hugged each other. "How do you know it was my mom?" I asked the counselors.

"It was said that Lena C. called on behalf of her daughter Misha Cruz and the other five students, and she caused quite a stir."

"Yeah, that's Lena. She's no stranger to causing a stir if necessary."

I spoke with Lena that same day and thanked her for her help.

"I let them have it, Misha! I love you. Be safe and call me when you get to Vermont."

And just like that, the tide turned again in our favor. I left Job Corps with such fond memories and a few friendships, too. I was ready to go to the next level. Job Corps prepared me in ways that helped build my confidence and independence.

At 17 years old, I was climbing, moving, and progressing. All this happened two years after Mom's death. God was guiding me every step of the way; I didn't always pay attention or notice the depth of His specific guidance and favors upon me.

As the van drove away from Cassadaga Job Corps, I looked behind me, filled with happiness and appreciation for the wonderful people I had encountered and all the goals I had set and accomplished for myself. I didn't know what lay ahead of me at Southern Vermont College, but sometimes the thrill is in not knowing.

Chapter Nine

Southern Vermont College

The campus of Southern Vermont College was a vast and charming estate that had belonged to Edward Hamlin Everette, a philanthropist and founder of the Bennington Museum in Bennington, Vermont. I arrived in the summer and immediately enrolled in a few classes after locating my room on campus. It reminded me of dorm life at Job Corps, except we could have loud parties and drink alcohol in the dormitory.

There were under 20 minority students, including myself, enrolled at the college in the summer of 1982. I met and became friendly with each of those students. Despite our different cultural backgrounds and places of origin, we understood each other. The vice principal was an African American man that we all loved. He was very approachable and offered support with whatever we needed. I was the youngest in our small circle, yet it was easy and felt comfortable engaging with the diversity and mixed cultures.

Bubba and CJ were senior students and arranged the trips and activities. Bubba worked in the mailroom and introduced himself to me while touring the campus.

"The student body is hosting a camping trip near Lake George this weekend. The bus leaves at 7 AM, hope to see you there."

"Oh yeah, I'll be there. I love camping!"

By the time Saturday came around, I was ready, and at the bus station before 7 AM. It had been two weeks since my arrival and I was going camping with a bunch of juniors and seniors. We drove just over an hour to Lake George. CJ asked if we wanted to go canoeing before setting up at the campsite. Unanimously, we hopped off the bus and rented canoes. Floating along the lake was so peaceful and the best way to enjoy the area and surrounding lake.

We reached the campsite and set up the tents by noon. Zain was from Jamaica, wore dreadlocks and the coolest sunglasses. He considered himself to be a Rastafarian, a religion that believes in Jah, as a single God that also lives within everyone. He showed us where we could find the bathroom and invited a few of us to explore the campgrounds with him. Nancy wanted to go with us, but she was in the middle of making burgers.

"Wait guys, let's eat first."

That was a great idea. I was starving, and the smell of the burgers was all I could think of. Nancy was a Caucasian girl from Long Island, NY. She was 5'9, blondish, and her native wit was perceived as attractive but unintelligent. In her case, this wasn't an accurate description. She was a senior and in fact one of the top students in her class. I really appreciated her steady, warm, kindness towards everyone.

Once the burgers were done, we ate, drank, sang, and danced to Reggae, Rock-and-Roll, and, of course, Rhythm and Blues. By nightfall, the men made a campfire, and we indulged in more spirits and songs. The stars were extremely bright and seemed closer to the earth. I don't ever remember seeing stars so bright and clear in Brooklyn. Perhaps the quiet stillness of being among nature allowed me to pay attention. Whatever it was, I marveled at God's incredible creation.

The next day, some of us rose early and went on a trailwalk. Others were hungover and slept in. It was our last day, and I wanted to explore the area. The New Yorker in me couldn't resist the opportunity for adventure. CJ announced the bus would depart at 11 AM sharp and told us not to stray too far. We returned and ate breakfast, then headed back to the campus.

I shared a room with a girl from Haiti. Her name was Julie. Her accent was distinct and made me think she was from the Caribbean. She was easygoing and laughed at everything. She was also a junior and spent most of her time at the library. I took three courses; the one I remember most was a Cross-Cultural Survey class.

We went on trips and participated in a few activities for that class. Our first trip was to a Renaissance festival. The costumes, historical setting, food, and shops mesmerized me. I wondered how something so culturally different and unfamiliar could do that. I didn't feel uncomfortable or anxious to leave. In fact, I took part in some activities and had the best time doing so.

As I reflect on my childhood, I grew up with many different cultures in my neighborhood. I guess that's one reason why this class trip was easy and accepting. We spent a day at a live concert in Sarasota Springs and attended a play at a local fair within the community. As the summer came to an end, I received passing marks in English 101 and Sociology, and my final grade for that class was a B+.

Glimpses of Will appeared in my mind as I was encountering different cultures and life experiences. I wanted the love of my life to be with me on what I believed to be a wonderous journey and so I called the Red Cross to try and locate him. They told me that I could send them a letter with Will's name, date of birth, and my relationship to him but it might take several weeks before they could gather info and locate him. I rushed to the post office after the call and sent the letter, stating that I was his concerned fiancé. I felt relieved that I had taken action to find him. Yet waiting for the reply was agonizing.

The noise, frequent parties, and chaos that naturally occurs in dorm life made me think about living off campus. I met Doris in my sociology class. She was from New Hampshire. Doris was medium height, brunette, and wore glasses. She had the deepest dimples too, a pretty girl with a calm and gentle demeanor. After class, we chit-chatted, and she asked me if I wanted to walk with her to the mailroom because she wanted to post an inquiry on the bulletin board for a roommate.

"Doris! I'll be your roommate. I've been thinking about moving out of the dorm. How much is the rent?"

"Really? Are you serious?"

After discussing the details, she took me to the apartment to make my final decision. The apartment was furnished with one bedroom and a spacious living room. It felt cozy, and the owner lived next door. It was also walking distance from the campus.

"I like it, Doris. When do you need my half of the rent?"

We both let out a hearty laugh and the following week, I moved into the apartment. It was the first time I had lived on my own, and it was thrilling. Doris and I took turns cooking and ate together most of the time. We had a similar temperament that made it easy for us to get along. We alternated sleeping in the bedroom. The living room had a very comfortable sofa bed and so I didn't mind forfeiting my turn when Doris' boyfriend Rob came to visit. He was tall, with short blond hair and steely blue eyes. They were a handsome couple. He was well-mannered and a gentleman. I liked Rob and could tell that he loved Doris.

In late October, Will's cousin Kelly called me and said their family received a letter from the Red Cross stating that Will had been in the Philippines for the past two years and would be returning to the states in a few weeks. I told Kelly that I had sent a letter to the Red Cross inquiring about Will. My heart started beating quickly with excitement from hearing the news. Kelly said the Red Cross informed Will that there had been an inquiry about him by his family and accomadations were made for him to call them from the Philippines. Kelly spoke with him.

"He wants to see you, Misha."

"I want to see him, too. I miss him so much."

"Thanks for the good news Kell! Give everyone my love."

"Will do Meesh, take care!"

I hung up the phone and stared out the kitchen window. I was barraged with thoughts and mixed emotions. Would we still have a connection, chemistry, love…? My trance was broken when I heard the key in the door. Doris walked in, greeting me with a warm smile.

"What's happened? You look like you saw a ghost?"

"Will is coming home from the Philippines next week."

"Oh-my-God. That's great news! Wait, isn't its great news, Misha?"

"The best news ever D. I'm just conflicted and still processing the info."

We stood in silence for a moment. I could feel Doris' eyes glaring as I turned away and looked out the kitchen window again. I heard her prepare dinner and as we ate, we talked about a hundred different subjects that didn't include Will.

The week of Thanksgiving Will came to Vermont to visit me. Before he arrived, I paced around the apartment, looking around to see if anything was out of place. I looked in the mirror a thousand times, making sure my hair and outfit was good. Doris went to stay at Rob's house for a few days to give Will and me time alone.

Ding Dong, Ding Dong.

"Oh, no. He's here!" I took a quick look at myself again, walked over to the door, and opened it. Screech! Bang! Crash! Boom! Butterflies fluttering as I looked at his tall, handsome, smiling face. We rushed toward each other and embraced in the doorway. He came inside, leaned in, and kissed me gently.

"You're still beautiful."

I didn't realize how much I missed and was still in love with him until that moment. We ate a nice meal and spent the entire night catching up on the lost time between us. He told me how proud he was that I was in school and trying to make a way for myself. I, too, was extremely proud of him serving and sacrificing for our country. Our relationship picked up where it left off. It seemed that we were destined to be together. He was the first man I ever loved, and I adored him. I was certain that we would marry and start a family.

Finals week was approaching, and I had a major decision to

make regarding my living situation. Doris and Rob got engaged, and he asked her to move in with him. Initially, Doris planned to leave our apartment after winter break, but changed her mind and decided to leave before the break. Most of the students I knew were content with dorm life or they were already renting an apartment, and so I told Doris that I would return to the dorm after break. I was happier for Doris and Rob than being sad about losing my independence. Will and I had rekindled our relationship, and it felt so right.

I left Vermont on the day of my final exam. It was exciting to return home after being away for the past seven months. I spent a few days with Lena and Dorian, then visited my siblings in Brooklyn. My plan was to spend Christmas and the new year with Will. He shared an apartment with a military buddy in Queens.

Three days before Christmas, we decided to go see a movie in Times Square. *Scarface* with Al Pacino was sold out and so Will bought tickets for the next showing. In the meantime, we went to Chock Full O' Nuts, a well-known restaurant that was located on 44th and Broadway. We ordered, and as we waited for the food to arrive, Will leaned across the table and gently held my hands. He looked at me and said he had something to tell me.

I thought, oh no. I mean, oh yes! He's going to tell me he wants us to get married. The waiter brought our food and asked if we wanted anything else before he left. I placed my napkin on my lap, smiling, anticipating Will's proposal. I picked up the utensils and gazed down at my plate.

"I'm bisexual," he said in a low voice.

I kept my head down, looking at my plate. "I know you are."

I thought he was joking and played along, but I heard his fork hit the plate.

"How did you know?"

I felt a lump in my throat, realizing that he was very serious. "I didn't know, I thought you were joking."

He said "something" happened while he was in the military. He didn't go into any details about what happened, and I didn't ask.

He continued. "I liked the experience and started seeing him. We were stationed at the same location, but before I returned home, I broke off the relationship with him."

I'm certain he saw the bewildered look on my face.

"Misha, I'm still attracted to women and I love and want to be with you."

I felt extremely calm. The moment was surreal, and I remained silent until a question popped into my head. "Are you sure you're completely over the relationship with that guy and want to have an exclusive relationship with me?"

He replied with an emphatic, "Yes!"

We left the restaurant, saw the movie, then headed back to his place. We woke up the next morning as though nothing had changed. However, I wasn't intimate with him. He prepared himself to leave for work and asked me to meet him later for lunch. I agreed. He kissed me and left.

An hour later, someone from an agency called the house phone, asking to speak to Will. When I said he wasn't home, the person asked if they could leave a message. I grabbed the nearest thing to write on. When I hung up, I realized I had written on an envelope that had a greeting card inside. I took the card out of the envelope and saw a picture of Garfield on the front with boxing gloves on. I opened it up and started reading the contents.

"Mush, Mush, Mush, here we go again! I'm sorry!' signed Ron. No date written inside, and the envelope was blank. Did this guy hand the card to Will in person? Was he lying about ending the relationship? What did all this mean? My head was spinning. I threw the card on the desk, sickened by what I had read.

Will called at noon and said he had made reservations at a restaurant near his job and gave me the address. I showered, got dressed, and put the envelope with the card inside my bag before leaving the house. When I arrived at the restaurant, I gave the host my name, and he escorted me to a table with a nice view of the park.

A few minutes later, Will walked in carrying a dozen red long-stemmed roses. I stood up, and he greeted me with a tight hug and kiss before handing me the gift.

"So beautiful, thank you, Will!"

We sat down and I asked him how his day was going. The host came to the table and took our order.

"An agency called for you and wanted to leave a message. I wrote it down on this." I reached into my bag and placed the envelope on the table. He brought the envelope closer to himself and sat back in his seat. We sat awkwardly in silence as he peered at the envelope.

"I've not communicated with him since you and I got back together. I received the card when I ended things with him."

"This situation is more complicated than I initially thought," I said calmly.

He tried reassuring me, but none of this made sense, nor did it feel right in my gut. I vaguely remember us eating something before he stood up.

"Can we discuss it later? I have to get back to work, baby." He kissed me on my forehead and told me to order whatever I wanted. Confused, I grabbed my roses and went back to the apartment.

Will's roommate, Eric, stopped by to pick up some clothes. He was going on a weekend trip with friends. Will introduced us, then asked Eric to stay for dinner. He accepted, and I listened attentively as they shared military stories about the good, bad, and tough times they had experienced. It was midnight by the time Eric left and by now, Will and I were too tired and not in the mood to address the elephant in the room. I stopped being intimate with Will the day he told me he was bisexual. HIV/AIDS deaths in the US had reached an all-time high, and I knew this was something to pay attention to. I hadn't fully processed his situation and needed to sort out my own thoughts and feelings.

The subject of homosexuality behavior was taboo in the Catholic religion, society, and the cultural era I grown up in. It was considered a death sentence if a man declared or presented himself as gay or bisexual. I felt more concerned about the health ramifications of the behavior of homosexuality—I knew people who had contracted HIV and some that were dying from the disease, and it scared me immensely. That fear overruled my emotions. My love remained deeply for him, but I knew that I didn't want to risk contracting AIDS.

I woke up at 4 AM, put my sneakers on, and told Will I was going for a walk. He got up and came with me. We walked to a nearby park. Suddenly, I felt an overwhelming wave of emotions in my body that caused me to shake profusely. With tears running down my face, I let him pull me close and squeeze me tightly against his body. I was grief-stricken by the news of Mom's death and, now, by Will's confession. I broke loose from his grip and started to walk briskly away from him. He kept pace with me.

"Misha, we can still plan our future and have a family. I never stopped loving you!"

I stopped abruptly and shouted angrily, "Why did you do this to us?" I was wailing miserably. He wrapped his arms around my body and held me tightly.

Memories of the way we were before he went into the military played over and over in my mind. My body softened and I put my arms around his neck. I felt his body tremble and knew that he, too, was in pain. Simultaneously, we pulled away, and he kissed me softly on the lips, then gently took my hand and we walked back to his place. I fell asleep in his arms, emotionally exhausted.

The sound of his phone awakened us abruptly at 7 AM. My eyes were still closed when he answered. I heard him going back and forth about something. "She's here with me. I told you it's over!"

I opened my eyes and stared at the ceiling, continuing to listen to the exchange as Will's voice rose with anger. In a split-second, I knew I didn't want to be a part of this dilemma. I got out of bed and started gathering my belongings. Will hung up the phone.

"Where are you going?"

"Back to Jersey."

"Wait, I'll walk you to the subway," he said.

As we walked and got closer to the subway stairs, a feeling of calm came over me. I had a premonition that my relationship with Will had come to an end. We'd been through tough times, but I believed no matter what happened, we would find our way back to each other. Until now. I was not equipped, nor capable, mentally or emotionally, to handle the complexity of this situation.

I hugged Will for a long time on the stairs of the subway. I didn't want to let him go. Instinctively, I knew it was the last time I'd see him. With a cheery face, I stepped back and started walking up the steps.

"I love you, Misha!"

Fighting back the tears, I turned around and said, "I love you too, Will."

When I reached the top of the steps, teardrops fell uncontrollably. I walked over to a corner near the turnstile to compose myself. I paid my fare, walked onto the platform, and waited for the train.

After that day, Will and I never saw each other again.

Chapter Ten

The Call

It was two days before Christmas, and I told Lena that I was returning to Vermont.

"Returning to Vermont? You should be home with your family, Meesh. What's going on? And what about Will?" she asked, puzzled.

I wasn't ready to talk about Will. I needed to be alone to clear my head, and frankly, I had nothing to celebrate. Returning to Vermont was the perfect retreat for me to exist alone.

When I arrived, my college looked like a ghost town. I walked towards the dorm and saw one of my classmates, Claudette. She was from the Bahamas, a beautiful girl with smooth brown skin, dimples, and light brown eyes. She was travelling that day to the Bahamas for Christmas. She had a small, quaint apartment close to the dorm. I asked her if I could stay at her place until after winter break and she agreed.

I walked into a festively decorated apartment, which reeked of holiday cheer. The small Christmas tree sat in the center of the dining room table. Colorful blinking lights and tiny ornaments covered the tree. More lights and small spray-painted snowflakes adorned the windows in the living room.

I heard a bell ringing from a nearby church at around 8 PM. It reminded me of how Mom used to attend midnight mass on Christmas Eve. Oh, how I missed Mom. It was lightly snowing, and I sat on the couch for a while staring at the colorful, blinking lights on the tree. It helped me get out of my head by focusing on the colors, size, and shapes of the bulbs and the synchronizing counts between each blinking light.

My concentration was broken by the growling in my stomach. I got up from the couch and looked in the cabinet: microwave popcorn. I turned on the TV, surfed the channels, and came across Eddie Murphy's standup comedy performance, *Delirious*. I can use a good, hearty laugh, I thought, and for the next two hours I ate popcorn and laughed my ass off.

Christmas day was peacefully still. I put on my coat, opened the front door, and stepped outside to a winter wonderland. I looked around and saw a few houses on a hill with colorful, blinking lights and inches of thick, heavy snow in the background. The scene looked like the perfect holiday postcard.

I felt content being away and alone in my version of a sabbatical. I breathed in the crisp winter air before going back to the house. I spent the next few days reading books and contemplating everything that had transpired over the past two years.

Students returned to campus after the New Year. I tried to focus and get back into that life but was having a very difficult time concentrating. My headspace wasn't where it used to be, and I was easily distracted and scattered. With hindsight, I should have gone to counselling or sought guidance to deal with my traumas. I hadn't fully grieved or talked about the loss of my mom and how the end of my relationship with Will had affected me. In addition, I lacked stability, structure, and parental guidance. As a result, I decided to leave school, move back to Jersey, get a job, before coming back to Vermont.

I returned to Teaneck before Spring Break and immediately found a job at an international bank in Midtown Manhattan in the check processing department. My one objective was to build up a good savings and get my own place. Lena required that I contribute $70 every two weeks from my paycheck towards room and board. I guess this was her way of teaching me about responsibility and paying my way. I had a positive experience sharing an apartment and expenses at school, so I understood the value of the lesson. My living situation with Lena and Dorian hadn't changed since I came back, except Dorian was living in my old room and I slept in his smaller room that led to the attic, where the squirrels occasionally appeared.

The Central National Bank was my first real job. In the beginning, I worked as a file clerk through a temp agency. Three months later, one of the check operators left the department, and the supervisor asked me if I wanted the permanent position. I was thrilled and accepted the offer on the spot. The next day, I began training as a check operator. I worked between 10 to 12 hours a day. We were given a car transportation voucher if we worked past 8 PM, which was a nice perk.

Lena was dating a man from Brooklyn; whose name was Brian. He had a few family members that had converted to Islam. I had an awkward encounter with one of his brothers who called from prison. I answered the phone, and an operator asked if Lena or Brian would accept a collect call from John. I hesitated because neither of them was home at the time.

"Yes, I'll accept the call."

"Hello, Lena?"

"Hello, this is Misha, Lena and Brian aren't here now."

"Misha, yes. My brother told me about you. I'm sorry for the loss of your mother."

I thanked him and expected to end the call, but instead he mentioned that he was a Muslim and his religion was Islam. Then he asked me if I knew anything about Islam. I replied that I did not. He offered to mail information to me and suggested that I speak with his mother or one of his sisters because they too had converted to Islam. Respectfully, I accepted his offer to mail the information. However, I had no interest in knowing or learning about Islam.

My family was Catholic. Mom used to have us read passages from the Bible once or twice a week and sometimes she asked questions about the passages, or we'd have a big discussion about what we read. We went to church every Sunday, and if Mom couldn't attend, she made sure that Phil and I did.

Long ago, a profound incident had occurred that increased my belief in God exponentially. I had a stomach-ache that worsened when I got home from school. Mom gave me medicine, ginger, honey, and peppermint tea to drink. Nothing worked, and I felt miserable and was in a lot of pain. Mom looked hopeless.

"Honey, I've done everything I can think of to help your tummy ache. Now, go to your room, kneel down, and ask God to take away the pain from your tummy."

Moaning and rocking, I answered Mom by nodding my head 'yes' and went to my room. Bawling my eyes out, I dropped to my knees, raised my hands up, and asked God to take away my tummy ache several times, then I laid on my bed and closed my eyes. I put both hands on my stomach, rubbing it gently, rocking from side to side.

Suddenly, the intensity of the throbbing lightened and just stopped. My eyes widened, and I lay very still, trying to figure out what was happening. I pressed my stomach inward and felt no pain. I turned my body right and left to see if the pain shifted. Finally, I lay on my stomach and felt nothing: the pain was completely gone! I jumped out of bed and ran into Mom's room.

"Mommy, it worked! God answered my prayer and made my tummy ache go away." I demonstrated by poking my stomach inward with force.

"God will answer when you ask Him," Mom laughed and hugged me.

Despite my solid belief in God, I hadn't turned to Him or the church very often to cope with unresolved grief and occasional bouts of depression. Outwardly, I appeared to be functional and balanced in my daily routine of work, exercise, and relationships. The truth of the matter, however, was that I was emotionally unstable. I managed these feelings by hanging out at the clubs, drinking, and partying hard. Almost anything that involved adventure, risk, or danger was acceptable to experience, I told myself unapologetically. At the time, I was unaware of how my life was spiraling out of control, until one evening when I took my reckless behavior to another level.

Melissa and I hadn't spoken since I returned from Vermont, even though we lived around the corner from each other. We reconnected when I started working every other weekend at the call center. She was a supervisor during the shift I worked. Early one evening, before our shift was over, she invited me and a few other co-workers to her house. We all accepted and followed her there. Melissa lived in a modern Tudor style home. It was white with black trimming on the outside. The living room was massive, with white furniture and carpeting. Obviously, her parents loved the color white. Melissa walked behind the bar and asked, "Alright, let's get this party started. What's everyone drinking?"

I blurted out, "Black Russian."

Others requested Hennessy, Sex on the Beach, and Tequila. There were a bunch of neatly rolled joints on the counter of the bar. I grabbed one and lit it up while waiting for my drink. The stereo system was set up on the other side of the living room. Melissa asked one of our co-workers, David, to DJ.

It wasn't long before the weed, alcohol, and music had us laughing, dancing, and talking loudly. Melissa's Mom and Dad came into the living room. She had on a long white silver fox mink coat. I'd never seen anything like it. Stunning, I thought. She greeted us and said that they were going to a club in the Village to see an upcoming singer named Whitney Houston. I'd never heard of then. Shortly after her parents left, Melissa went behind the bar and pulled out a large amount of cocaine and some pipes.

I had tried cocaine before at the club, but never with a pipe. We walked over to the bar and watched Melissa turn the powder into a solid rock, then she showed us how to smoke it from the pipe.

"This is free-basing," said Melissa. "Who wants to try?"

What the hell is freebasing? I thought. The few people I saw at the clubs smoked weed from those pipes. At least that's what I assumed, until now. Everyone took a pipe off the counter, a small rock from the bowl, and started smoking. When I inhaled the smoke into my lungs, I instantly felt a rush of energy to my brain, then a sense of alertness and excitement. The feeling of being high was on another level, and truly addictive. I wanted more and more. We ended up smoking the entire night.

It was 7 AM when I left her house. My brain was wired and fried at the same time. When I walked in my front door, Lena was sitting in the breakfast nook drinking tea and reading the newspaper. I said good morning and went straight up the stairs without waiting for her reply. I didn't want to have a conversation with her in my current state of mind. I plopped down on my bed and closed my eyes. My body was exhausted, but my brain would not shut off. I got up, took a shower, and went down the road to the deli and bought a turkey and cheese sandwich along with a bottle of orange juice. I walked back to the house and started eating the sandwich, hoping that my high would come down.

I heard the house phone ring, then Lena shouted for me to pick up the phone. On the other end was the Muslim guy, John, from prison.

"Hi, Misha, how are you doing?"

"I'm good, thanks," I said, rolling my eyes.

"Did you get a chance to speak with my mother or sister about Islam?"

"No!" I replied, annoyed.

I was not in the right headspace to speak with him and politely excused myself by thanking him for checking on me, then hung up the phone. I finished the sandwich and lay down, still wired, but felt my mind and body trying to get in sync.

I heard the house phone ring again. Lena shouted for me to pick up.

WTF! I snatched the receiver, "Yes."

On the other end was a girl from my old neighborhood in Brooklyn. Her name was Kim. She was several years older than me, so we had never hung out. However, we shared the same birthday, which made our relationship special.

Kim came from a good family, well-liked around the neighborhood. She had an older sister, Terri, and two brothers, Brandon and Sam. The last time I saw Kim, she was dating an IBM software developer named Scott. He seemed to like her a lot. I always seemed to see him either picking her up or dropping her home from a date.

"Hey, Misha! It's Kim Marshall."

"Kim, it's nice to hear your voice. Oh God, it's been years since we've spoken."

"Many years. I ran into your brother Phil and asked for your number. Are you busy?"

We caught up with the past and current events in our lives as she told me that she had married Scott and they had two children. I congratulated her and expressed my happiness to hear they had started a family together.

"He died a year ago."

Dismayed, I cried, "Kim! I'm so sorry for your loss. What happened?"

She explained how two years before his death, he went to California for two weeks related to work. While there, some co-workers invited him to a party and introduced him to free-basing cocaine. He quickly became addicted and hid it from her for a long time. His behavior changed, and it affected everyone around him. He finally told Kim what had happened in California and said he needed help. He went into rehab and it worked for a short time, then he relapsed and got worse.

Early one Sunday morning, he returned home after being out all night. Their children were in the living room watching cartoons. She asked him if he wanted something to eat. He replied, "No. I'm sick of being like this." He kissed her and said he was going to take a shower.

Kim said after she made breakfast, she realized he had been in the shower for more than 30 minutes. She called his name and knocked on the door. When he didn't answer, she opened the door and saw him hanging from the ceiling with a belt tied around his neck. She called 911 and asked a neighbor to take her children. When the paramedics arrived, her husband was pronounced dead at the scene.

I was stunned and speechless for a few seconds. Was I in the Twilight Zone? My thoughts raced. What were the odds that I'd spend the entire night into the early dawn free-basing cocaine after being introduced to it for the first time, only to receive a call from a family friend who I hadn't seen or spoken to for more than eight years? Who, by coincidence, runs into my brother, gets my number, and conveys a story of how the use of freebasing cocaine led to an addiction that ultimately caused her husband to end his life?

When I ended the call with Kim, I sat at the edge of my bed, completely clear-headed, pondering over the two calls. This was a clear sign and direct warning from God for me to change my path or possibly face a similar consequence.

I decided to call John's mother and sister to ask them questions about their conversions to Islam. I also wanted to go visit a few Masjids while in Brooklyn to inquire about classes for non-Muslims, to learn about Muslims and the religion of Islam.

Chapter Eleven

The Path to Islam

"And Allaah found you lost, and He guided you."
(Surah Ad-Duha 93:47)

I went to a Masjid in Brooklyn called At-Taqwa, where there were many Muslim women dressed in loose-fitting clothing who wore large scarves covering their heads. They had a separate praying area from the men. When I entered, I saw some women praying and others reading. One woman came over to me and asked warmly if I needed help. I told her I wanted to learn about Islam. She said they had classes twice a week for non-Muslims to learn the basics of Islam and another Masjid called Al-Farooq had Tawheed classes.

"What is Tawheed?" I asked.

"It is the belief in the oneness of God."

Belief in the oneness of God, I repeated to myself as I walked out of the Masjid. Oneness of God. What did that mean? I started to examine the concept of the oneness of God and what it meant in Catholicism, but quickly realized that it wasn't the same. Catholics believe in the divinity of Jesus as son of God.

They also recognize the trinity, that the father God, the Son, and the Holy Spirit are together as one God. This couldn't be the same belief, or was it? Such questions piqued my curiosity about the Tawheed class, and so I jumped on the train and headed to Masjid Al-Farooq to find out when the class began.

I met two Muslim men as I walked into the lobby of the Masjid. One of them turned towards me and asked how he could help.

"I heard there is a class being taught here about Tawheed."

The other man looked up.

"Yes, there is. My name is Amir and I'm the teacher of that class. What would you like to know?"

I told him I was Catholic and knew nothing about Muslims or Islam but wanted to learn more about the religion.

"Tawheed is the foundation of Islam and the first principle of learning and understanding about the belief in the oneness of God. You'll need this book for the class." He pulled a book out of his briefcase and showed me the cover, *Kitaab AT-Tawheed*. He told me I could buy it next door at the Islamic bookstore. He said the class was interactive, and he encouraged the students to participate, complete homework assignments, and prepare for weekly quizzes, then do a final examination once we had completed the book. I expressed my eagerness to start the class and thanked him for taking time to explain everything.

"May Allaah open your mind and guide you to the correct way." He excused himself and walked towards a group of men waiting to speak with him. As I walked past them, I heard Arabic being spoken. I looked back and saw my teacher, who was African American, having a conversation in Arabic. I felt proud and honored to meet someone from my culture that had mastered a difficult language like Arabic. It left a huge impression on me.

I went next door to the bookstore, purchased the book, and jumped on the train to Port Authority, where I caught the bus back to Jersey. As I looked out the window and saw us leaving the city, making our way onto the George Washington Bridge into Jersey, I contemplated how I was about to transition from a chaotic, hectic state of mind to one of calm and order. I closed my eyes and felt a release of tension from my body, replaying the details of my trip to the Masjids, and, specifically, my encounter with Amir.

When I arrived home, it was dinnertime. I sat and ate with Lena and Dorian, then quickly went up to my room and started reading Kitaab AT-Tawheed. The first chapter was called AT-Tawheed, [The oneness of Allaah]. Two verses from the Quran started the chapter: Allaah the Almighty said, "And I [Allaah] created not the jinns and men except to worship me alone." Surah Ad-h-Dhaariyat 51:56, and in the next one He stated, "And verily, we have sent among every Ummah [community, nation] a Messenger, proclaiming, 'Worship Allaah alone and avoid [or keep away from] Taghut'" [all false deities, that is, do not worship deities besides Allaah]. Surah An-Nahl 16:36.

As I went on to read two additional verses from this short chapter, I was drawn to the understandings taken from the verses above, at the end of the chapter:

1. That the wisdom behind Allaah's creation of jinn and mankind is that they worship Him alone.
2. Allaah's complete independence from His creation.

3. Evidence that humanity has not been neglected and left without guidance.
4. The universality of the message to all nations, and the fact that the message brought by each new Messenger [Prophet] abrogated that of the previous Messenger.
5. That the mission of the Messengers was to call the people to the worship of Allaah and to reject all false deities.

I was intrigued by what I read and wanted to dive deeper into this subject of Tawheed. I also wanted to gain information about how to perform the five daily prayers, the reason behind it, and to know who Muhammad was and what made him a Prophet. I decided to attend Masjid At -Taqwa, and Tawheed classes with Ahmed at Masjid Al-Farooq.

Shortly after attending the classes, I bought Islamic clothes and practiced the prayer at home secretly. I hadn't told anyone about my studies of Islam because I wasn't sure if I wanted to live my life as a Muslim and I wasn't yet ready to give up partying with my friends and hanging out despite feeling drawn to what Muslims believed and the way lived.

Amir was a principal of a school, before becoming an administrator for the Board of Education in New York City. He was a renowned educator with a unique way of simplifying complex Islamic subjects. I understood from the book in our Tawheed class that the creed of Islam is to single out God for singular worship without associating partners to Him. God doesn't have a son, and He didn't create people in His image. He's not the sun, moon, trees, fire, stones, or cows. There is nothing like or comparable to Him and He is alone in His

Lordship, not in need of any partners, helpers, or associates. He's completely sufficient.

According to Islamic creed, if one were to believe that God has a son or that He has qualities, attributes, and resembles His creation, then it's equivalent to blasphemy and complete disbelief in God. This was opposite to the creed of my Catholic upbringing. How can this be, I wondered? Although most religious entities believe that God exists, there seems to be great divisions between religious creeds when it comes to how one believes and worships God.

After learning about the Islamic creed, I was convinced it was the correct way to believe in and worship God. My questions were answered, and my heart felt naturally drawn and accepted this creed of Islam. One afternoon, after the basics of Islam class ended, Khadijah came and asked me if I was ready to become a Muslim. She asked me this question after every class and my reply was always 'no.' Except this time I responded, "I'm ready."

She looked surprised and excited. "Before you say the Shahadah [testimony of faith], I'll ask you a few questions. Do you believe that Jesus was a Messenger [Prophet] of God and not his son?"

"Yes," I replied.

"Do you understand, accept, and have a firm belief in the Islamic creed, belief, and worship in the oneness of God?"

"Yes," I affirmed.

She turned to the women in the class and asked them to witness my declaration of the shahadah. She faced me and said to repeat after her. "Ashadu an la ilaha illa illa-ilah, wa ashadu anna Muhammadan rasul ullah." This means, I bear witness there is no

God [deities] worthy of worship except Allah [God] and I bear witness that Muhammad is His slave and Messenger [Prophet].

"You are a Muslim! As salaamu Alaykum [peace be upon you], my sister."

"What do I say back to you?" I asked.

"Wa alaykum as salaam [and peace be upon you]."

The women came over to greet and introduce themselves to me. I sensed genuine happiness and most of them gave me their numbers and told me to call if I needed or wanted anything. I left the Masjid feeling confident that I had made the right decision to become a Muslim. I was ready to continue learning and studying my new way of life.

The next day, I woke up early to prepare myself for work. I wore a gray, long, loose-fitted skirt that flowed down to my ankles, a beige oversized blouse, and wrapped a large light gray scarf around my head. I walked downstairs and saw Lena. Startled, she said. "You're going to work dressed like that?"

"Absolutely," I said confidently and told her I had become a Muslim while at the Masjid. I ignored the look of displeasure on her face, smiled, and told her I'd see her later.

When I arrived at the bank and walked into my department, everyone froze when they saw me. I said good morning as I passed by the cubicles. My supervisor and two co-workers in my section just stared at me. After a few seconds of total silence and shock, my co-worker asked if I was feeling sick. I laughed and told them I felt well and that I was a Muslim, and this was the dress of a Muslim. The supervisor tried to smile, but it was apparent that she felt awkward about my appearance and didn't know what to say.

After a few hours went by, some girls from another section in our department came to speak with me. They asked a lot of questions about Islam and couldn't believe that I was covering up my hair. At the end of the conversation, they respected my decision to change my religion, and our relationship at work never changed. The department manager came to our section, looked right at me, and motioned for me to come with her. We sat down in her office and she bluntly said, "What the hell is going on with you?"

"Nothing. I changed my religion to Islam and want to live my life as a Muslim. Is my Islamic dress going to be a problem while working here?"

She shook her head. "Your religious choice has no bearing on keeping your job. I'm orthodox Jewish and there are a few similarities between Islam and Judaism."

I thanked her, stood up, and walked out of her office. I completed my first day as a Muslim at a major international bank and didn't get fired or ridiculed. That assured me I was on the right path.

I started spending more time with my classmates at the Masjid after the Tawheed class. The subject fascinated me, and I couldn't get enough. Midway through Kitaab AT-Tawheed, Amir stayed after class, answering our questions, and helped us learn the Arabic alphabet. By the time we completed the Tawheed book, I had memorized the Arabic alphabet myself and was able to read a few words.

Amir started another class after we finished the Tawheed book called *Tajweed Made Easy*. Tajweed is from one of the sciences of the Quran that applies a set of rules for the correct pronunciation of the Arabic letters and their qualities necessary for reading and reciting the Quran.

A few months into the class, Amir had us each take turns reading a page of the Quran. I really wanted to learn the Arabic language and how to read the Quran perfectly, like Amir. We asked about his experience living and working in Saudi Arabia and, more importantly, how he had become fluent in Arabic. He told us to read from an all Arabic Quran without translation every day. He said reading Arabic in the Quran was key to becoming proficient readers, and the study and practice of Tajweed would perfect the pronunciation of the Arabic letters, thereby perfecting the recitation. I listened to the best Quran reciters to hear the correct Arabic pronunciation and started memorizing chapters (surahs) of the Quran.

The next day, I started carrying an all Arabic Quran with me and read from it every day. It was difficult for the first few months, but then I noticed my reading started flowing and it took less time to read a page. I looked up words in an Arabic dictionary that I didn't understand and was totally engrossed with learning to read the Quran.

During this time, there were a few American Muslim men that went abroad to study Arabic and other sciences of Islam for the purpose of returning to the States to teach. Some got accepted and received full scholarships to study at the University of Madinah in Saudi Arabia, while others opted to take the more traditional path of studying in the Masjids with great scholars in places like: Egypt, Yemen, Morocco, Syria, Mauritania, Malaysia, and Indonesia. I admired the students' knowledge and attended their lectures and workshops. I watched them in awe, teaching subjects from Arabic books and translating them into English.

I read and memorized a few small surahs in the Quran, but I didn't understand what I had read or memorized without looking at the English translation. I heard about a great scholar who created an environment of learning in a valley in Yemen that had male and female students from all over the world, travelling and living there to study Arabic, Quran, and a variety of Islamic sciences. I wanted to be a student seeking Islamic knowledge in an environment like that and often prayed to Allaah to make a way for me to do it.

Islam has five pillars that every Muslim is obligated to fulfill throughout their life;

1. The shahadatain [The two testimonies of faith]: The statement by which a person enters Islam, "I bear witness that nothing has the right to be worshipped except Allaah, and I bear witness that Muhammad is the Messenger of Allaah." The first statement negates worship for everyone and everything other than Allaah, while affirming that worship is for Allaah alone, without partners. The second statement affirms Muhammad is the Messenger of Allaah, thus his statements are believed, and his commands are followed.

2. The prayer: Muslims pray five times a day. The prayer is the connection between man and his Creator.

3. Zakat: Zakat is a form of charity taken from the affluent and given to the needy. Each year, the individual is

required to give 2.5% of his savings to the poor within his community. The poor are not required to pay Zakat.

4. Fasting: Ramadhan is the ninth month of the lunar calendar. While fasting, the person abstains from eating, drinking, and sexual relations from daybreak to sunset. Fasting trains the soul to patiently abstain from what it desires and naturally craves. Fasting brings about compassion and empathy for those who go without food and water throughout the year due to poverty. Those who are sick, elderly, and unable to fast are excused.

5. Hajj: Hajj is the pilgrimage to Makkah. Muslims are only required to perform Hajj once in their lifetime, if financially and physically able. Hajj contains many spiritual and social benefits. Muslims of all races, colors, nationalities, and economic backgrounds, from kings to laborers, unite in one place, dressing in uniformity, to worship their Creator.

I'd been a practicing Muslim for ten years and as I reflected upon the peaceful and stable life Islam provided, I couldn't have been more content, which made me think of Will. A few months after I became a Muslim, I ran into his cousin, Bernie, while visiting a friend in the hospital. Bernie was a police officer and embraced me warmly despite being surprised to see me dressed in Islamic clothing. I asked about Will, but he said it had been a long time since the family had seen or heard from him. A year after that, I was told by someone close to me that they saw Will at a distance coming out the subway carrying a women's handbag. Whether it was true or not, I felt concerned about his health and often wondered over the years if he had contracted HIV/AIDS and died. It wasn't meant for he and I to ever cross paths again, a wisdom that lies with Allah. Before Islam, Will was a pillar of strengthen and support for me during a time of total chaos in my life. More importantly, he was the absolute love of my life and he'll always be remembered that way.

Chapter Twelve

Journey to Hajj

In 1992, I married a Muslim man, DJ from Brooklyn, who had three small children from a previous marriage. I was familiar with him from mutual friends in the community, and he was known to be a good man. He was a conductor for the New York City Transit Authority.

One afternoon, I waited on the platform for the train and when it came, the doors opened, and DJ stuck his head out from the conductor's window. We looked at each other, surprised, then laughed because the day before my sister and I had run into him at the mall. It seemed like we were supposed to meet again.

He came over and greeted me, then asked for the number of my wakeel. A wakeel is typically from the male relatives of a woman, who will ensure that the proposed groom is reliable and a trustworthy person that will fulfill his responsibilities towards the future wife. In Islam, a man will contact a woman's male relative to express his interest in marriage to her. The male relative will ask the woman if she's interested or not. If the woman agrees, then arrangements are made for the two to have a chaperoned meeting to talk and ask each other questions. This process can be shorter or longer; it depends on the two people getting to know each other. There is no dating or pre-marital relations before marriage, and so this is how it's done.

DJ and I married and had a nice wedding at the Masjid. We moved to a one-bedroom apartment in Kew Gardens, Queens and settled into married life. I got pregnant about two months after and unfortunately, had an ectopic pregnancy two and a half months later. It was my first time being pregnant, and I felt sad about the loss. The surgeons came into my room after surgery and told me that despite losing a lot of blood, my ovaries were healthy and intact. That was very good news and made me feel grateful to Allaah for getting me through the surgery successfully.

DJ and I moved to New Jersey to be a part of a growing Islamic community that offered us more opportunities to learn and study Islam. His children lived with us during the week and visited their Mom on weekends. DJ was a great father and provided well for our family. There were challenges with his ex-wife that lasted most of our marriage. They had three children, and she wasn't quite over him. I didn't realize this at the time, but by the time I did, I felt enervated.

In 2001, I had the opportunity to perform the pilgrimage [Hajj], the fifth pillar of Islam. It requires travel to Makkah, Saudi Arabia to perform a series of rites over a period of five days. I was elated when DJ came home and said that his supervisor gave him the time necessary to perform Hajj.

I prepared myself a few months before by working out with weights and ran extra miles on the treadmill to build my stamina and strength. Performing the rites of Hajj requires strength and endurance. Millions of people are there doing the rites at the same time and so being mentally and physically prepared is important.

We had 25 people in our group, and I was very excited when we got on the plane. It wasn't my first flight, so I felt comfortable throughout the 11-hour ride. We stopped in Athens, Greece and had a nine-hour layover there. Luckily, the Hajj package included an eight-hour tour of Athens. The tour bus took us to the Parthenon first. It was a famous ruin that I didn't find very interesting, but I still enjoyed being in the city of Athens.

We saw an ancient Greek theatre and the Panathenaic stadium. When the tour guide told us that it was the first Olympic stadium, a few of the men in our group pretended to be Olympic track and field stars and ran around the stadium a few times, as we all had a good laugh at them. Our final stop before dinner was to a museum that I don't remember the name of. What I do remember was most of the exhibited sculptures were of men with their small private parts exposed. My friends and I laughed the entire time.

Our last stop before heading back to the airport was to a Greek restaurant. It was great eating authentic Moussaka and a Greek salad from where such cuisine was invented. Once we arrived at the airport, we had 30 minutes before our flight took off to Jeddah, Saudi Arabia. My friends and I went to the souvenir store but were unable to buy anything because every item showed or was made from a private part. The Greeks loved their private parts.

Our group arrived in Madinah first and stayed there for five days before going to Makkah. Mountains surrounded the city, and it had a desert feel despite the many modern hotels and restaurants in the area. There was a noticeable smell of bakhoor [scented wood chips] as we entered, and a calm and quiet unlike any other place I've ever been. Madinah is the second holiest city after Makkah. The Prophet Muhammad (peace be upon him) migrated to Madinah and his Masjid, Masjid An Nabawiyah, was the third Masjid built in the history of Islam and now the largest in the world.

Adjoining the Masjid is the "Green Dome" called The Rawdah [The garden]. It's a place that refers to the area between the tomb of the Prophet Muhammad (peace be upon him) and his pulpit. It is a place of immense spiritual and historical significance. Pilgrims visit and attempt to pray there either before or after they perform Hajj. It's widely believed that supplication and prayers uttered there are never rejected.

The atmosphere in the city of Madinah was serene and tranquil. The most memorable moment I experienced happened when I went to The Rawdah. I wasn't feeling well. My throat was sore, and my body achy. I prayed and sat for a while supplicating, asking Allaah to remove the sickness so I could perform the rites of Hajj in a healthy state. I heard the evening athaan [call to prayer], and after a few minutes, I stood up for the prayer and heard the voice of one of my favorite Quran reciters.

My heart was filled with emotions of happiness and gratitude because it was such a rare opportunity to be led in prayer by one of the top Quran reciters in the world. When the prayer was over, I started walking towards the door and noticed that my throat wasn't sore and my body no longer achy. I turned around, went to the prayer area, and prostrated, thanking Allaah for answering my prayer. I visited Madinah a half dozen times thereafter and each time I prayed and supplicated in The Rawdah, Allaah answered my prayer swiftly.

We made Umrah [a shorter version of Hajj] upon arrival in Makkah. I was speechless when I saw the Kaaba. Prophet Ibraheem [Abraham], a man of monotheism [the belief that there is only one God] who fought idolatry, built the Kaaba with his son Ismaeel [Ishmael]. It's a building made of stone that can neither bring harm or benefit, meaning we don't worship the Kaaba or believe that it can answer our prayers or bring us good or steer us from evil or harm. Instead, we know that it is Allaah alone who answers prayers, brings benefit, and protects from evil and harm. The Kaaba is the symbolism of Tawheed [the belief in the oneness of Allaah].

Putting on an Ihram [an unstitched white cloth that men wear] is necessary before performing Hajj or Umrah. Women wear regular clothing and it involves being in a state of purification and sanctity. We began the Tawaf [circling the Kaaba seven times in an anti-clockwise direction] that starts and ends at the location of the black stone, which is set inside of the Kaaba. Supplication and reciting the Quran is done while going around the Kaaba. Then two short prayers were offered, before we proceeded to the Sa'y: walking and shuttling between two hills called Safa and Marwa seven times and ending at Marwa. Umrah, and the state of Ihram, ends with clipping the hair. Men can shorten or shave their heads and women clip their hair one or two centimeters.

There are more steps involved with the rites of Hajj that happen over five days. Two days before the rites of Hajj began, our group was told that a famous religious scholar from Yemen was going to give a lecture at someone's house. Immediately, we piled inside a small bus and arrived shortly at the house. I could hardly contain my excitement.

The women went into a room and listened to a short talk given by the scholar's wife, while the men sat in a courtyard listening to the lecture of the scholar. During the talk with the scholar's wife, I whispered to my friend, Sumayyah, that I was going to the courtyard to peek at the scholar. In our eyes, Muslim religious scholars were like rock stars, and Muslim women rarely got an opportunity to see them. This was an opportunity of a lifetime and so I quietly stood up from the talk and walked out to the courtyard, as Sumayyah followed.

There were curtains around the courtyard, blocking our view. We walked towards the curtain, found an opening, and peered through it. I saw a short, white-haired man sitting in a chair at the front of the circle surrounded by men attentively listening. Sumayyah and I stood there gazing with great reverence at the scholar. Suddenly, the curtain started to fall, and we ran back inside the house, cracking up. Once we returned to the hotel, we stayed up until 4 AM, telling our story to the other women in our room. It was an incredibly special experience.

In the morning, we gathered our belongings and headed to a place called Mina [city of tents] to sleep overnight. It's literally a city of tents that looks like a gigantic cloud on the ground and the place where the Hajjis gather to prepare to start the rites. Mina is a big, open outdoor area like a camping site with 100,000 air-conditioned white tents, each one roomy. Ours fit our group comfortably.

The next day began with the rites of Hajj, starting with praying all day on Mount Arafat. The day of Arafat is the most important rite of the Hajj. It's a hill surrounded by wide open space. The Hajji's pray, read Quran, repent in the area, and hope to have all of their sins removed if accepted by Allaah. I went away from my group and found an area near the hill to focus and spend all of my time conducting acts of worship by myself. It was the best feeling in the world.

In the evening we went to a place called Muzdalifah and stayed overnight, then in the morning, we returned to Makkah to circle the Kaaba seven times, followed by walking and shuttling between the two hills called Safa and Marwa. It took us much longer to do these two rites because there were many more people, and we were smashed together like sardines. I was mentally and physically exhausted once we completed the rites on this day.

The next two days involved figuratively stoning the devil in Mina. We picked up small pebbles and threw them at a tower, then we paid for an animal sacrifice, and the meat was distributed to feed the poor. The rights of Hajj and Umrah are complete with clipping the hair.

Despite the mental and physical challenges of performing the rites of Hajj with four million people, it was emotionally and spiritually cleansing to my soul and the best experience of my life. It elevated my faith, love, and connection to Allaah. We stayed in Saudi Arabia for a month and I didn't want to leave. I was in a Muslim country that constantly reminded me of Allaah and fully supported my way of life. I cried the entire plane ride home and was determined to figure out a way to return there or to some other Muslim country.

A month after I returned from Saudi Arabia, I had an epiphany. After going through much adversity and trials, I realized that there is good and benefit in everything that happens in one's life. The death of Mom led me to Islam. Islam saved my life and replaced everything I lost with something exponentially greater.

There may have been some initial resistance from her about my conversion to Islam. However I believe that after seeing how my daily life revolved around the remembrance and worship of God and how my practice was directly attributed to the foundation that she initiated, her resistance would have further dissipated.

My siblings have remained accepting, respectful, and supportive from the beginning of my conversion to Islam. I think they may have thought I was going through a trend and wouldn't stay the course, but my living abroad in three different Muslim Countries for ten years removed their doubts about how serious I was about Islam. I left the U.S in 2005 and returned for the first time in 2015 when my nephew, Aris, graduated from high school.

We attended his graduation and then ate lunch at a beautiful waterfront restaurant in Long Island City. It was a festive, long overdue siblings' reunion. Whenever the four of us got together, it seemed we picked up wherever we left off, without a lapse in time or space, and it's always a grand hardy time.

Before traveling back to Egypt, I gathered with my siblings again in New York to celebrate my nephew Aris' graduation from college with a degree in Robotic Engineering. During my visit, I was able to spend time with each of them individually. Our conversations are usually reflective of the storms we faced as kids and most times reminiscent of Mom. My brother Phil lives by the creed of perception, "It's all about perception, the way you see a thing will determine the effect it has on you."

We've never wavered in our love and closeness with one another over the years, despite the many obstacles and odds against us. I'm so incredibly proud of us and of the positive impact we each continue to contribute to various sectors within society. As I stare out into the Mediterranean Sea from my balcony in Alexandria, Egypt, my mind and soul are at peace knowing that my siblings and I continue to carry Mom's true warrior spirit as survivors and declared victors of her battles.

Made in the USA
Middletown, DE
22 May 2022